A LITTLE BIT

OF

INTUITION

AN INTRODUCTION TO
EXTRASENSORY PERCEPTION

CATHARINE ALLAN

STERLING ETHOS
New York

STERLING ETHOS

New York

An Imprint of Sterling Publishing Co., Inc.
1166 Avenue of the Americas
New York, NY 10036

ISBN 978-1-4549-4089-0

Distributed in Canada by Sterling Publishing Co., Inc.
c/o Canadian Manda Group, 664 Annette Street
Toronto, Ontario M6S 2C8, Canada
Distributed in the United Kingdom by GMC Distribution Services
Castle Place, 166 High Street, Lewes, East Sussex BN7 1XU, England
Distributed in Australia by NewSouth Books
University of New South Wales, Sydney, NSW 2052, Australia

For information about custom editions, special sales, and premium and
corporate purchases, please contact Sterling Special Sales at 800-805-5489 or
specialsales@sterlingpublishing.com.

Manufactured in China

2 4 6 8 10 9 7 5 3 1

sterlingpublishing.com

Interior design by Kennedy Liggett
Cover design by Elizabeth Mihaltse Lindy
Illustrations by Shutterstock.com: sunlight77 *(tattoo eye)*; satit_srihin *(border)*

CONTENTS

INTRODUCTION

We all have intuition, whether or not we are conscious of it.

When I wake up in the morning and reach for my alarm clock every day, I don't marvel that I have a hand that knows how to press the snooze button—but I am aware on an instinctive level that I have a hand and that it's intact and serves me.

Intuition is like this too. You *know* more than you realize. It is more than just instinct. It operates in the background of the mind. There are so many small decisions you make every day, all day, based on information you are sensing but don't necessarily make conscious.

If you want to go out to eat and are walking along the street contemplating which place is best, you are most likely getting a vibe of each possible option. You know on some level if the restaurant feels warm, clean, welcoming, or smells good. You can walk in and sense how the experience of eating there will be. When you aren't aware of what you are sensing in the environment, intuition is still operating on the subconscious level. Often people will just say they "aren't feeling it," or they are getting a good or bad vibe from a place or person, and they leave it at that without going into why.

When you make the "why" conscious, you are accessing the subtle realm of intuition. Almost anything can be perceived when you become aware of those vibes. The word is colloquial, but it has a basis in science. In the words of Albert Einstein, "Everything is vibration." It's true. That vibe you are getting is a holistic readout of energy, and as you develop and understand how to open and use your intuition to guide your life, you will be able to receive more and more information that is intuitively accurate and detailed.

How do we know when the information or vibe we are sensing is accurate? How do we know it isn't just our imagination, fear, or fantasy? How do we learn to tell the difference between receiving a true message or vision? And once we *do* learn and trust our intuitive gifts, what do we do with them next?

Developing your intuition is a deep journey into the nature of reality, and it is at times a painful journey to awakening—but it is very often a magical journey as well. *It is the path to true self-trust.* It can bring you into greater flow and ease, synchronicity and manifestation, and sometimes it can save your life.

We live in a very uncertain world. Even if there is and has always been great change on the planet, we could argue that right now we are in a very intense time of change once again. We need to know how to trust ourselves now more than ever as societal structures, such as basic human rights and laws that have been fought for, are being challenged or erased, and the speed at which technology has altered the way we relate to each other—or don't—has accelerated. Our values, as well as our environment, are under threat. As we rely more on technology and have less direct social contact, intimacy seems to be more challenging, and the resulting anxiety and loneliness are heartbreaking. In order to retain or restore our capacity to connect, we need to be open.

Opening your ability to trust yourself and read situations well, or navigate intuitively when you don't have full information, is not entertainment or a game of predictions. Training yourself to trust your intuition and read the vibration of what is going on around you helps you make wise and strategic choices in life and keeps you adaptable in times like ours. By using your intuition, you stop looking outside yourself—to authorities or news media—for the truth, and instead you go within and know it from your own direct experience.

I will show you how.

❊1❊

WHAT IS INTUITION?

IF I WERE SITTING WITH YOU RIGHT NOW ON A PATIO overlooking a main street with many people passing by, I could easily show you how much of your life includes intuition that you may not even realize. I could ask you, as you watch a person on the street below, for your first impression, and you would instantly have one. It is usually some singular thing you notice, and then you quickly make a decision to engage—to look more, or to be curious about the person—or choose to avoid. Most people choose to avoid and not "analyze" their intuition after that. If I pressed you to say why you chose to be curious or to avoid this person, you might be surprised by what information you picked up intuitively to guide your decision.

I could ask you, "Is this person healthy? Is he or she single? Does she or he make a good income? Does he or she have many friends? Would you feel safe with this person? Would you trust this person?" And you would be able to answer me quite quickly based on those first impressions. How could you know so much about a stranger on the street without meeting that person and knowing them for enough time to see patterns or verify your assumptions? Some may call this instinct; some may call it intuition.

If I pressed you even farther and asked you what details you sensed that led you to come to those conclusions, you might see visual evidence from which you gleaned information—such as posture, type of dress, cleanliness, level of self-care, and the amount of overall confidence the person projected. However, after years of training people to trust their intuition more, I can tell you that many of us sense information about people that has no visual evidence, *and* we tend to reach consensus on our respective first impressions; in general, intuitives don't have wildly varying readings.

How many times have you kicked yourself because you felt or intuited something about a person that turned out to be right in the end? You might end up saying, "I knew he would back out of this business partnership," or, "I had a feeling there were a lot of issues with her family." Most of us have these initial gut feelings—and we either don't make this conscious to ourselves *or* we feel guilty, as if we are prejudging someone before knowing them. There is a big difference between profiling people based on visual cues such as gender, race or color, and age and using our intuitive system to feel the overall energy of a person's character. It can be a slippery slope until we know we are receiving our intuitive guidance versus projecting a fear, prejudice, or similarity between people/scenarios related to memories, but it can be discerned with training. When I ask you to sense if a complete stranger is happy, healthy, lonely, or feels safe to you, this has no race, gender, or religion associated with it.

Everyone has a slightly different idea of what intuition is or isn't. Different religions and philosophies reference intuition and regard it as anything from indigestion to a gift from the divine. Some define it more cognitively or scientifically, and others take it to the realm of metaphysics and paranormal abilities.

Our society is still very much under the influence of rational thinking and analysis. When a subject or issue has been approached rationally, we feel secure that emotion did not get in the way to sway us. But we are visceral, feeling beings. If we cut off the branches we still have a tree, but a compromised tree that has to regrow again. There is a place in society for everything, including rational and clinical analysis. Thank goodness for it! We have made many advances because of it. However, it is not the answer to everything in life, since it misses a huge part of who we are. If we learn to hear and observe our intuitive process—in a scientific way—now we have a super tool for arriving at more holistic behavior. We need to start observing our intuitive process and learn to know our own sensations and cues when they are accurate. We will see patterns over time that prove to be correct, and then we'll recognize these sensations again in the future. By not addressing emotion and denying it as a factor in everything we do—we are like the branchless tree.

BUDDHISM

Buddhism has for centuries helped people to discover the true nature of the mind and develop practices to observe and calm both mind and body. It isn't a system of worship so much as a search for truth, and this seems to open the door to other parts of our experience and consciousness.

The Buddha said, "It is natural that doubt should arise in mind. I tell you not to believe merely because it has been handed down by tradition, or because it had been said by some great personage in the past, or because it is commonly believed, or because others have told it to you, or even because I myself have said it. But whatever you are asked to believe, ask yourself whether it is true in the light of your experience, whether it is in conformity with reason and good principles and whether it is conducive to the highest good and welfare of all beings, and only if it passes this test, should you accept it and act in accordance with it" *(Kalama Sutta, Anguttara Nikaya)*.

Asking yourself if something is true in the light of your own experience is telling people that they are their own authority, including over God or any other deity. This places the power and light back into the hands of each person. You own your own perceptions. This opens the door to also trusting our intuitive perceptions once we learn how to perceive correctly.

According to Ajahn Sumedho, one of the senior Western representatives of the Thai forest tradition of Theravada Buddhism, in his book *Intuitive Awareness*, "There is a huge difference between the use of the mind to think, to analyze, reason, criticize, to have ideas, perceptions, views and opinions, and intuitive awareness which is non-critical.

"In contemplating right understanding (*samma-ditthi*) I like to emphasize seeing it as an intuitive understanding and not a conceptual one. I have found it very helpful just contemplating the difference between analytical thinking and intuitive awareness, just to make it clear what that is, because there is a huge difference between the use of the mind to think, to analyze, reason, criticize, to have ideas, perceptions, views and opinions, and intuitive awareness which is non-critical. It includes criticism; it's an inclusive awareness. It's not that criticism isn't allowed in it, criticism is included; so the critical mind is seen as an object. This is the tendency to criticize or compare, to hold one view, to say that this is better than that, this is right and that is wrong, criticism of yourself or others or whatever—all of which can be justified and valid on that level. We're not interested in just developing our critical faculty, because usually in countries like this it's highly developed already, but to trust in intuitive awareness (*sati-sampajanna*)."

The concept of "inclusive awareness" he mentions is a beautiful way to describe intuition. When we have a strong gut feeling, a flash of intuition, a sense of just knowing—it takes in multiple aspects all at once and bypasses the analysis or criticism. The black-and-white thinking or the self-doubting line of questions is gone and there is a more holistic sense of a situation, person, or place. We may not perceive every detail of it, but we can get a global and true reading of it on a core level.

Ajahn Sumedho continues: "*Sampajanna* is a word that is translated into English as 'clear-comprehension,' which is so vague and even though it says 'clear,' it doesn't give me a sense of the broadness of that clarity. When you have clear definitions of everything, then you think you have clear comprehension. So that's why we don't like confusion, isn't it? We don't like to feel foggy, confused, or uncertain. These kinds of states we really dislike, but we spend a lot of time trying to have clear comprehension and certainty. But *sati-sampajanna* includes fogginess, includes confusion, it includes uncertainty and insecurity. It's a clear comprehension or the apperception of confusion—recognizing it's like *this*. Uncertainty and insecurity are like *this*. So it's a clear comprehension or apprehension of even the most vague, amorphous, or nebulous mental conditions."

This is a very important aspect of intuition and developing ourselves to hear it. We need to accept that foggy or nebulous vague space in ourselves. Sometimes intuitive information isn't literal. The sensation we get, the insight that comes, is not rational or definable. It doesn't mean it's inaccurate just because we can't verbalize it in a literal way. This is why it gets very frustrating to some and difficult for others to listen to and live with their intuitive awareness. There is a lot of inner work to accept the varying states of mind, emotion, and quality of insight before we can master it and use it as a tool.

PLATO

Philosophers also attempt to define the nature of reality and existence, so it's only natural that we would find descriptions of intuition here. As much as modern society would like to omit or demote our intuitive faculties, these guys knew it was an important part of us.

Dr. Garth Kemerling, in his online guide to western philosophy (philosophypages.com), quotes translations of Plato's *Republic* on the various states we evolve to. He takes us through the four stages outlined by Plato.

> "[O]ur apprehension of reality occurs in different degrees, depending upon the nature of the objects with which it is concerned in each case. Thus, there is a fundamental difference between the mere opinion we can have regarding the visible realm of sensible objects and the genuine knowledge we can have of the invisible realm of the Forms themselves. In fact, Plato held that each of these has two distinct varieties, so that we can picture the entire array of human cognition as a line divided proportionately into four segments. (*Republic* 509d)

> "At the lowest level of reality are shadows, pictures, and other images, with respect to which imagination or conjecture is the appropriate degree of awareness, although it provides only the most primitive and unreliable opinions.

This would be the stereotypical way intuition and psychic abilities are portrayed as being scary, vague, psychotic-induced images that are unreliable, or as complete flights of fantasy—again unreliable as intuitive insight and clarity. It is in this part of the description we would see someone projecting what they fear or desire onto a person or outcome that has nothing to do with clear perception or objective intuition.

> "The visible realm also contains ordinary physical objects, and our perception of them provides the basis for belief, the most accurate possible conception of the nature and relationship of temporal things."

This is the tangible world we are all used to and rely on. If I can see it, I believe it.

> "Moving upward into the intelligible realm, we first become acquainted with the relatively simple Forms of numbers, shapes, and other mathematical entities; we can achieve systematic knowledge of these objects through a disciplined application of the understanding."

This includes the study of mathematics, geometry, astronomy, astrology, and anything conceptual. This is where we need some reasoning, logic, and ability to see patterns, perceive in the abstract world, and calculate or postulate based on theorems.

"Finally, at the highest level of all, are the more significant Forms—true Equality, Beauty, Truth, and of course the Good itself. These permanent objects of knowledge are directly apprehended by intuition, the fundamental capacity of human reason to comprehend the true nature of reality."

Plato places intuition at the top of the chain of human perception! Through intuition we can access higher truths and concepts and integrate them to comprehend the "true nature of reality." We can't get a higher endorsement than that—or can we?

ISLAM

In his book *Knowledge in Later Islamic Philosophy: Mulla Sadra on Existence, Intellect, and Intuition*, Ibrahim Kalin writes, "Ibn Sina returns to intuition and explains its role in logical syllogisms. At the end of his discussion, he refers to intuition as a 'prophetic capacity' and calls it a 'sacred capacity.'" He goes on to say, "[I]t is the highest faculty of prophethood. It is more appropriate to call this ability a sacred capacity. And this is the highest degree of human capacity [to know]."

This swings us to the other extreme of how intuitive capacity is seen—as a gift bestowed on only some to use for prophetic reasons. I believe we all have some degree of intuition, just as we can all sing. We aren't all opera singers though. Some of us are bestowed with intuitive ability as our main talent. However it can be developed more by everyone willing to learn how.

Before we begin that journey, though, we really do have to look at two major figures in our modern culture and how they saw intuition, because their thinking has underlined our experience for the past century.

SIGMUND FREUD

We see in Freud the embodiment of strict discipline applied to psychology and its consequences. In *Sigmund Freud: His Life and His Mind*, author Helen Walker Puner writes, "Ordering his life like a precision instrument, he believed that all men must so order themselves. He knew that he had sacrificed pleasure. 'Science,' he once said, 'betokens the most complete renunciation of the pleasure-principle of which our minds are capable.'"

You can see where we get so much of our perfectionism and our pleasure-denying attitudes from if we follow his ideals. You can almost taste the shame inherent in the words. This level of self-denial doesn't lend itself well to intuition, and yet Freud admitted late in his career that he must have also used his own "intuition and guesses" in his free-association method.

Puner goes on to say, "The fact is that at the core of all Freud's work, under the masses of detailed clinical observation, is the intuitive power, the 'guesses' if you will, that set the whole scientific system in motion. Freud knew that the source of his intellectual strength and prowess lay in those natural gifts and inclinations which characterize every philosopher, and which in the end boil down to 'intuition,' 'speculation,' to the charge of 'unfounded,' 'unproven' and 'undocumented.'"

We can see how rigorous he must have been in wanting to prove and quantify that which is very difficult to do, and in that pursuit deny his own intuitive and speculative influence. Much of this underlying speculation and aversion to intuition and lack of proof seems to come from his influence—of course not entirely, but he colored our thinking for generations.

Intuition, as we saw in our previous examples, has a more gentle and organic feel to it. It's very hard to hear the true inner voice of intuition when imposing so much judgment on our process and person.

CARL JUNG

In his work *Man and His Symbols*, Jung writes, "Imagination and intuition are vital to our understanding. And though the usual popular opinion is that they are chiefly valuable to poets and artists (that in 'sensible' matters one should mistrust them), they are in fact equally vital in all the higher grades of science. Here they play an increasingly important role, which supplements that of the 'rational' intellect and its application to a specific problem. Even physics, the strictest of all applied sciences, depends to an astonishing degree upon intuition, which works by way of the unconscious (although it is possible to demonstrate afterward the logical procedures that could have led one to the same result as intuition)."

Here it is significant to note that he acknowledges that intuition can also be part of science.

He discusses intuition more when talking about transcendence, saying, "The bird is the most fitting symbol of transcendence. It represents the peculiar nature of intuition working through a 'medium,' that is, an individual who is capable of obtaining knowledge of distant events—or facts of which he consciously knows nothing—by going into a trancelike state.

"Evidence of such powers can be found as far back as the Paleolithic period of prehistory, as the American scholar Joseph Campbell has pointed out in commenting upon one of the famous cave paintings recently discovered in France. At Lascaux, he writes, 'there is a shaman depicted, lying in a trance, wearing a bird mask with a figure of a bird perched on a staff beside him. The shamans of Siberia wear such bird costumes to this day, and many are believed to have been conceived by their mothers from the descent of a bird. . . . The shaman, then, is not only a familiar denizen, but even the favored scion of those realms of power that are invisible to our normal waking consciousness, which all may visit briefly in vision, but through which he roams, a master.'"

Here we get to intertwine two great minds of mysticism and symbolism—Jung and Campbell. Both allowed space for intuition and beyond. Their work has helped us break free of the problems that come from the rigidity imposed by some science, religion, and psychology. We are so much more!

I would define intuition as the capacity to *know*.

When we can't quantify our knowing with facts, research, a linear train of thought, or logic—but we *know* something—this is intuition. Sometimes we have a sensation of knowing that is very simple, accurate, and helpful, which guides our decision making in a good direction. It can be as simple as a "yes" or a "no" feeling we get that comes suddenly and clearly. We usually feel it in our bodies somewhere. We call it a gut feeling for a reason. We didn't do any reading, research, analysis, or consultation with experts. We just *know*. We just feel the "yes" or "no" and act on it.

Other times intuition includes a lot more information that we sense or suddenly receive. It can come in the forms of the *clairs*: clairvoyance, clairaudience, clairsentience. It is the same sudden visceral feeling of knowing, but now it is broken down into the way we received it. Was it visual? That is clairvoyance. Was it auditory? That is clairaudience. Was it a physical feeling or emotion? That is clairsentience. There still isn't any research or logic applied to what you suddenly know, but now it is expanded to include details such as a flash visual, a word or name, or a specific bodily sensation or emotional state. It comes instantly and without trying or craving it. It literally walks across your mind and leaves. It can be a bit like waking up and having that last sweet feeling of your dream before *poof*—you're awake and it's gone. You have to trust what you remember and go into the detail of it to describe it. If you try too hard to remember or try to analyze what it means, it's lost.

I would also say intuition is a sensation.

Every intuition you get has a sensation attached to it, even if very fleeting and subtle. I see it much like deeper meditation. As you go deeper into your meditation practice, your awareness becomes more and more subtle. The sensations you feel are lighter, faster, and more specific. Your mind is calm enough to receive insight—that spontaneous awareness or knowledge or seeing of a pattern. In order to really hear your intuitive voice on a regular basis and live by it, your mind must be calm. You need to be in a deeper state of awareness and you need to know yourself well.

The preliminary experience of intuition might be an overall strong feeling that comes out of nowhere, but you suddenly know what happened, or why, or what to do next. The intuitive voice made its way through all the mental clutter and screamed at you! Thank goodness you listened (we hope).

The next stage of intuitive awareness might be that you see an increase in these kinds of experiences and now you are paying closer attention when they happen. You may not understand what is happening, or why, but you acknowledge that you are feeling and hearing your inner voice more.

The next phase may be that you now act on this growing awareness. You start noticing more synchronicities around you, and you see signs and symbolic messages everywhere. You may begin to guide life choices on your gut feeling or intuitive information and have more flow and ease. However, at the same time there is usually craving (looking for them and making them fit versus having an organic experience).

This is a slippery-slope stage in your intuitive awareness because you are now very excited to be awakening to a whole other paradigm where following your inner voice is leading you to new people and new realizations about yourself and the world. You feel connected and plugged in to a greater whole, as opposed to feeling isolated.

Some of the intuitive information you receive will be very accurate and help you and others. It is also the time when you can start seeing your strong ego make its way to the surface. You may desire or crave *more* of these experiences and sensations—and being *right*. At some point along the way to trusting your intuition on a regular basis and living your life by your own guidance, you *will* encounter your ego. Everything you sense or feel can seem to be coming from God or a Higher Power, Deity, Angel, or Spirit Guide, but you need to determine when intuition is pure and when you're just wanting it to be so.

The next leg of the journey to accurate intuition is discernment of messages, information, or sensations. Here the real inner work begins. You must know yourself well enough to say, "I have a strong gut feeling, but that is my trauma, PTSD, or projection versus a pure intuition or reading of energy." You can spend many years healing and finding your way through what is personally generated, compared to what is purely perceived or received intuitively.

Intuition is the capacity to know without logic, research, proof, or linear thinking. When you hone this ability that we all have to the degree that you can discern the various sensations and accurately interpret them, you are truly empowered and free.

2

MY JOURNEY INTO FULL SELF-TRUST

I BECAME A CLAIRVOYANT MEDIUM BY LEARNING HOW to trust my own intuition and follow it throughout my life. If you ask most experienced intuitives, mediums, or healers of any kind, they are likely to tell you their beginnings weren't easy. Most of us lived in some form of abusive environment, exile, or estrangement from our families unless we are the fortunate ones who had the support of a mother or grandmother who fought that battle too. I am no different.

Many years of hindsight and healing have shown me that many in my family of origin are also astute and intuitive as well. The difference has been perhaps my openness to take it farther and the conscious intention I set of healing—which leads to truth telling, which leads to pain or the polarization of those who don't want to heal on a deep level. Now that I'm in midlife, I see how much strain my path has placed on me and on my family. I don't think I could've changed anything much, though. Breakthroughs of awareness and healing have happened with some of my family members and changed their lives too. So when I share my early story I want to be clear, my intention is solely to give context, not judge anyone—because a lot of healing has taken place and continues to take place. Some things take a lifetime to heal.

I remember clearly as a child that people were hiding their truth. I could always feel they weren't being honest about how they actually felt, and everything was suppressed. Obviously, being that little, I didn't have words or a way to articulate any of it, so I had tantrums and displays of strong emotion. I also remember clearly one memory that informs the psychology of how I grew up. I was about five and was standing in our kitchen. I was about the same height as the table, and was looking at our huge clock with Roman numerals and a black border. It was close to bedtime. My mom was near the kitchen reading or knitting in her favorite chair, and my brother, two years younger, was in bed. Dad wasn't home yet. I remember looking up at the clock and asking, "Mom, what time is Daddy coming home?" and she may have said seven o'clock or something, and I sat and calculated how long I had left to feel safe and at peace before he arrived. Everything in my early life was a calculation of avoidance of him.

If intuition starts in childhood, it often begins in trauma. Think about it. If you don't feel safe, you have to read your environment and people well to keep yourself safe and comfortable. You learn to read the emotional pulse of everyone and you start trying to find strategies to keep things calm, or to please, or find ways to escape or get relief. When you're a child, you don't have the option of leaving, and you don't have the psychological maturity to process what is and isn't your fault. I grew up in a house of grief and narcissistic abuse. There is finally so much more written about the panorama of mental health issues, including narcissism, but this is a recent phenomenon. In the early 1970s in rural Ontario, when a doctor suggested family therapy after a tragedy, it was a big deal.

My dad and my mom both lost their fathers very young in life in their university years, and both always seemed to be grieving them but not talking about them. I could always feel this pain in my body and emotions, and the older I got, the harder I tried to get them to open up about their lives—to no avail. My mom is much better now that she has healed from narcissistic abuse, but when I was growing up it was an unexpressed, unnamed pain that permeated the household. It was the undercurrent beneath the masks of happy, high-functioning, community-oriented, and perfectionistic young teachers. And it drove me crazy.

When I was around five years old, my aunt, my dad's sister, Barbara, took her own life. She was a social worker who had gone to Africa in the 1960s—which I have utmost respect for. She was also bipolar, and she battled her illness for many years. At one point she went through the horrible electroshock therapy at the Allan Memorial Institute in Montreal, the city I moved to in 1991. I had no idea at the time of the move that I was connected to her history in that way. According to my dad, she often felt suicidal, and my grandfather would try to talk her through it. She was in a relationship with a man who was also struggling with mental health issues and who took his life a year before she did. She was only thirty years old when she died.

It's a necessary story to tell because, after that, my dad refused to get family therapy and held great resentment toward Barbara. He projected onto me her qualities and the blame he had for how her illness affected his life. He went so far as to say that her illness caused his father's death. She was too sensitive, artistic, always needing help. And yet she dedicated her life to helping people. He said I was just like her. I grew up thinking my sensitivity was going to give my dad a heart attack, afraid I was "crazy" too, and that I would also die at age thirty. There was no room to talk about this or her life. Everything was suppressed, and we were supposed to be "perfect" and keep up the image of a perfect family. I was told I "think too much," that my perceptions were wrong, or "maybe it's your period." I was battled all the time when speaking my truth and wanting to be heard. I fought back quite a bit in verbal debate, but out of fear I didn't take it too far. With the history of mental illness of my dad and his projections onto me, I was afraid of being put in a straitjacket or having my rights taken away if I pushed farther. And that began a chapter of duality for me, a time when I knew my perception and intuition were right—but it wasn't safe to share them. It took years to start opening up and healing from the fear of telling my story. So my journey through this trauma is partly how and why I learned to trust myself over all else that was going on.

By the time I was around fifteen, I could see through my dad's narcissism clearly enough to rebel. I had always seen it, but didn't have the words, maturity, or power to do anything. By age fifteen I saw through the manipulative tactics and didn't want anything to do with his guilt trips anymore. So shit sort of hit the fan. This was the first time I acted on my gut feelings and intuition. I *knew* I was right about him and that I should not give in to him. I didn't know there would be so much pain or fallout from rebelling, though. Rebelling in this case was more on a psychological level. I never ran away from home, I have never taken drugs, and I don't drink. I wasn't dating tough guys or failing school—I was at the top of the honor roll. So my rebellion was in not submitting to him as the narcissist wants. I had already endured years of brainwashing and gaslighting while stuck with him in daily car rides from school. At fifteen I was developing a intuitive strategy for how to live my own life smoothly, navigating around his moods and making choices that got me away from home. By seventeen I knew I wouldn't be spending summer breaks at home during my college years and I made sure I got steady 90s in school so I could get into any university I wanted. I chose a program they would support—and at the time thought it was my choice too. I made sure to apply to schools that were hours away so my father wouldn't just drop by and visit, giving me the freedom to start my own life. I emancipated myself. Reading every situation helped me navigate this emancipation smoothly.

There were many years of arguing with my mom about my perceptions. I had no idea I was intuitive or psychic. I was just saying and acting on what I saw and felt was true, and it got me into lots of heated debates with others. It didn't feel like a gift. It isn't a gift if others see it as a threat and no one points out that you have an ability. That came much later. Some of my first predictions were in high school. I was quite diligent as a student of my own intuitive or perceptive process. I would share my gut feelings and say what was "going" to happen to certain people when they announced decisions or started dating people, and so on. I would point out people's true intentions or true nature and got resistance all the way. Now, thirty-plus years later, some are seeing and saying the very things I perceived all along. So my intuitive journey at first was extremely frustrating and isolating. And yet, I *knew* I was right, and I honored this. I was disappointed and lonely that others couldn't see it too. After all, it wasn't to condemn anyone—it was to help them heal or improve their lives by telling them the truth. I lived my life by the motto that the truth sets you free, so I have always appreciated people telling me things I couldn't see that would make my life better. But as we all know, most people don't like that.

By late high school many of my observations and predictions about people's behavior, character, or events came true, and I once again argued with my mom, "See! I am not too sensitive. I was right!" All these years later I know now that the haze of gaslighting she was under made it almost impossible for her to see anyone or anything else clearly if it was too close to her. Now she does, and we have many good conversations. It took her leaving my dad and years of her own recovery process to bring us closer again. It has been very hard.

I bring this up because we often see books or websites where people with abilities don't talk much about the painful or isolating side of having these gifts. The path to fully trusting yourself when you have opposition and lack of support is not easy, but it is exactly by trusting your own intuition that you can navigate anything and save yourself! I have made it my mission in life to teach and guide others to trust themselves at this depth, so if you are ever in a similar circumstance—where you know something and are not believed or supported—you will also know that you are right and begin to emancipate yourself as well. There are always going to be situations in life that get complicated, or toxic, or where you are vulnerable to a narcissist or a sociopath—because they are among us. You will also run into complicated situations with friends, family, or coworkers, because humans are complex!

When I began to empower myself by believing and acting on my gifts, my path unfolded in magical and synchronistic ways. There was a bright light on the other side of the cloud.

When I applied to Queen's University for Concurrent Education, I knew I would get in. I had confidence and enjoyed the process of applying to universities. I was looking forward to a new life in Kingston! There were suddenly so many more aspects of life to navigate that, once again, my intuitive side was held in private. I didn't go around at Queen's truth-telling new friends—I'd learned those consequences—unless I felt it was essential for someone's growth or the health of a relationship. But I also lacked the healthy communication skills needed for that, so my intentions weren't clear to people and I lost friends.

The breakthroughs began to happen again when I realized that I was on my parents' chosen path and not my own and had to once again trust what my heart and gut were saying and once again strategize how to follow them.

I was in the middle of my college education when I applied for and received a small business loan for students. I used it to tap my creativity, to sew and craft items for a market stand in downtown Kingston. I had not felt so alive in years! I suddenly regained mental clarity, feisty creative spirit, and energy. I once again knew that I was on the right path. This feeling of aliveness was so real, how could it not be right? I decided after that to pursue design, and that meant quitting the university before graduating as a teacher. My parents weren't so thrilled but they supported me, which I'm grateful for. I decided to move from Kingston to Montreal after another adventure in self-trust and intuition.

In my third year at Queen's University in Kingston, Ontario, I lived in a house with five other students, but it wasn't going well socially. I felt totally left out among the people I thought were friends—a common theme and painful rite of passage for young adults away from home. I tried my best to make things better but I just wasn't happy. I felt so invisible that I said to myself, "I bet I could go away for days without telling them and they wouldn't even notice." So I did. I packed my best clothes and went to Quebec City for three days because I knew my soul needed the beauty and romance of the old city. I told no one I was going—not even my parents.

When I switched buses in Montreal on my way to Quebec City, there was a man sitting in the aisle seat beside me with the most angelic blue eyes I'd ever seen. He smiled once but that was it. When we got to Quebec City, I got off the bus and was a bit lost as to where to go for the hostel. He saw that I was confused and asked me in French if I needed help. My French wasn't good in those days. I said in English that I didn't know where the hostel was, and he walked me there. When I went inside and asked for a room, there was nothing left. I was pondering what to do next when he held his hands up in the air and said in a broken accent, "You can stay with me. I no touch." I *knew* he was kind and safe, so I accepted. Logic and fear and worry will always tell a twenty-year-old girl not to stay with a stranger—and I support that sensible choice. But I stayed because, even though I had never met him before, my intuition *knew* he was safe. I had grown up with a man who wasn't safe, and so I knew who was. He was a perfect gentleman for three days, taking me all over the old city, walking, dining, and shopping. We had a lovely time and were both learning to speak English and French. That experience has stayed with me in a positive way. Every so often the vibration is good, and you can do things that might be conventionally wrong—but it will be right for you, even magical. After that I knew the deep level at which I could connect with someone, and that men could be kind and true—even strangers. The amount of time knowing someone didn't matter in this case. We often *know* right away with people, and I trusted my intuition even more after that experience proved it correct.

On the way to Quebec City, we crossed the Jacques Cartier Bridge and I had a bird's-eye view of Montreal. I remember looking out the bus window at the sunny skyline and feeling a download of informational vibrations about the city. I once again *knew* that there was something special and mystical about it. I had a strong knowing that I could be anything here and it would be okay. When I got back home to Kingston, I began to look for design programs in Montreal. I knew I was going to move there.

During my Queen's University days, I kept my spiritual life to myself, but I studied astrology and observed people. This is something I've done since around fifteen years old. Every so often people would talk about it with me but I didn't bring it up much. During my last year of school I had a series of predictive dreams, including a vivid one about sitting in an amphitheater on stone benches. Three of us sat in a specific way and I could see what we all were wearing. I have kept a journal of my experiences and feelings (and rantings and worries, like anyone else) so I had it to refer back to years later when the dream manifested. After I left home, my inner life was no longer impeded and, in time, I came to see that my path as a mystic had begun. Many spiritual seekers live in a state of exile in order to experiment and go deeper within.

In 1991 I moved to Montreal to begin interior design courses at Dawson College. Of those at Queen's University whom I'd told about the move, some reacted with excitement and many with disdain. It showed me how a small decision I made in being true to myself brought out the true nature of those around me and revealed their true relationship to me. We all live this. When you trust the message intuitively and act on it right away, you bypass long periods of anxiety, conflict, or worry. I let go of anyone who wasn't happy for me since I knew I was on path, and this made room for closer ties with others.

When I went to visit Montreal at first to get an idea of the city and find an apartment, I had no experience living in big cities, let alone French-speaking big cities. I didn't speak enough French to feel at home yet. At one point I was in the middle of Rue Saint-Denis and East Duluth Avenue when I had an anxiety attack. There was too much energy and info coming through and I had no clue where to look or what direction to go in. I had to surrender and say, "Okay, I will stop apartment-hunting for now and just enjoy looking around. Something will pop up when I get my energy back. I turned down Duluth, because I could see beautiful architecture and I love that! Within ten minutes I saw a sign saying A LOUER—for rent. It was a gorgeous triplex with a stone facade and arches over the balconies in set stone. I knew I couldn't afford it and said, "What the hell, let's just look at it for fun." It turned out to be an agency! I went inside, and they helped me find an apartment that fit my budget and needs. They drove me around to see places. They negotiated my carpets, fridge, and stove and showed me the local market and where to get groceries. I was right beside the biggest fabric area in the city—and I had been sewing and designing since I was five or six! I felt like the universe had guided me. I didn't hear a voice saying, "Turn that way. Go into that apartment." I was simply compelled and followed my own intuition. Many of us are like this when we let ourselves trust. We all live synchronistic moments in life at times. You will live even more of them if you develop and trust your intuition.

The day I arrived in Montreal with my moving van and one friend, there were two girls playing on the sidewalk in front. I asked them where to park the truck and they said, "Can we help you move your things inside?" I was amazed at this generosity and said yes. I found out only at the end of unloading a big truck full of boxes that the girls were the daughters of the agent who helped me find the place, and she had asked them to come help me. I was starting to feel that Montreal was a blessed place to be!

Many things happened in a huge learning curve when I was living in Montreal because I had grown up in a sheltered—but lovely—area that wasn't really exposed to other cultures or languages. Part of me knew I was sheltered, and I didn't want to live that way anymore. I had no idea what I had wished for! Everyone kept advising me to get a French boyfriend and learn the language, but I kept meeting

Greek men. My first boyfriend in Montreal was from Athens and was studying at the same college. We met in gymnastics classes. He turned out to be a huge catalyst in my spiritual life, but I didn't really recognize that until years later.

Andy was a handsome, rebellious, and quirky guy who loved to debate things, play Dungeons and Dragons, climb things, and eat. He was twenty-two. He had tarot cards and one day pulled them out in his kitchen. For him it seemed to be another game, but I never put them down again. I bought my own shortly after that and started building my knowledge and switching my paradigm of life yet again. One day he told me he had a surprise place he wanted to take me to, so we went downtown and walked into Le Melange Magique the second year it opened. It was a metaphysical and pagan store. They had spiritual magazines, tarot card decks, specialized astrology books, and a huge apothecary of herbs for healing and spell-crafting. They made their own potions and incense and had a beautiful white cat named Kether living there. I was spellbound—quite literally. I went in again five years later when I felt ready to give readings to the public and was hired a couple of weeks later—to stay and build my abilities and my practice or business—and I stayed for about thirteen years.

While I was dating Andy, I had a few very strong trancelike predictive experiences. He lived with his sister, and her boyfriend was over a lot, as was I. I started to have prolonged déjà vu experiences. At first it happened around his sister, Anna. I would be semi-awake in the morning and hear her speaking to her boyfriend, getting ready for school. It was mundane—nothing dramatic, just daily life phrases, but I knew what she would say before she said it. It happened on and off for months. One morning I tested myself to make sure I wasn't making it up. And as I lay in bed, down the hall from her, I knew what she was going to say next, and she did.

Another time my trances surrounded Andy's friend Pete, who became a much longer story in my life than Andy—but I digress. He was one of the Dungeons and Dragons guys who came over every week to yell over dice together. At one point I was in a trance state knowing what everyone was going to say next and what actions were coming next, and I was right about it. It lasted for a few hours.

In the spring of 1992, Andy invited me to go to Greece with him for part of the summer. Of course I accepted! I had studied art history and architecture at the university and was studying design now, and was beyond excited for a chance to see Greece and be with him and his family there. At one point his sister's boyfriend joined us at his parents' place and he wasn't too happy. In fact, he opted out of going to see *Elektra* at the ancient theater of Epidavros, where Plato and Socrates would have given their discourses.

I was sitting there with Andy's sister and mother with the play about to begin when I had one of the strongest dream recalls of my life. It was the dream I'd had two years earlier, in Kingston, of sitting in an amphitheater with two other people. The locations where we were sitting, the clothing we had on—it all matched. I then had a sense of what was to come next in my life based on that dream. This has happened many times since—recognizing in the moment that I had dreamed it and knowing what would happen next. That was a predictive dream. I also believe, in the case of Greece, that it was related to a past life. Everyone surrounding Andy was giving me strong mystical experiences.

The next important part of Andy the catalyst was Miriam. Miriam worked with Andy at an all-night convenience store that had a bakery. She was making pastries and breads in the middle of the night while he scratched lottery tickets and sold cigarettes and gas. It was in the middle of nowhere to me—on a northern road that I never would've gone to otherwise. He insisted I meet Miriam because she was into astrology as well as art. So I consented and went out at three a.m. on a night bus to meet her. She was too busy to say hello, but I saw her face, and sat beside Andy until daylight, watching him trying to win the scratch-off lottery. Oh well.

A few weeks later when spring came, I stepped out onto my back balcony to get some air. I lived in those iconic walk-ups with spiral staircases and large back balconies overlooking the alleys full of laundry, old woodsheds, fences, and cats. This day I was outside just taking in the fresh air of the day when a woman stepped out on the balcony beside me. It was Miriam. She had been my next-door neighbor the whole time! She then became my mentor in astrology, cooking, and alley-shopping for anything you could restore. We did indeed have a lot in common.

Miriam lived with her husband, Paul, who was an architect, and she was a painter. They had lived in Europe for a while, where she learned a lot about cooking. She and I would hang out for hours and days talking about astrology, to the point that I became proficient at analyzing a chart and knew all the planets, sign combinations, aspects, and transits. I learned on my own how to cast an astrology chart by hand long before we had computer software to do it for us. Remember, this was 1992! She also taught me to make a mean tomato sauce with fresh Italian ingredients. We lived near the largest market in the city and had access to Little Italy as well. We walked those alleys many days and hours. She was hunting for old wooden frames—window panes with no glass left to turn into art canvases. I was looking for anything cool to furnish my apartment with and, later, my loft.

I can thank Andy for the many experiences and people he brought into my life that turned out to be instrumental in my spiritual path.

There was another mentor, a man I met who turned out to live in the apartment below Miriam! We had a strong connection, and I could feel it was on another wavelength from what I was used to but, once again, I couldn't have defined how or why. He was a healer. He had studied Reiki before I knew what Reiki was or practiced it myself. I remember speaking to him in my kitchen about my life, and he said he felt that I had a lot of energy that needed to be cleared—at twenty-two, I didn't really know what that meant yet. So there I was, once again with a man in an unfamiliar situation that defied logic—but I *knew* he was safe and true, and he was. He knelt down beside me with one hand a few inches from my backside and the other a few inches from my pubic area. Again, logically in unfamiliar situations like that, we would tell a young woman *not* to go there. But he was giving me Reiki and healing. He was lovely and he listened to my pain that came up strongly after such a clearing. He was a gentle Scorpio. It would be about twenty-one years later that I was told by a medium in Sedona, Arizona, that I needed to learn Reiki to allow the energy to come through me, not *of* me. I now use Reiki in my work all the time, and it has been life changing.

I never went looking for teachers and at that time was not trying to cultivate my gifts or read books about tarot readings and Reiki. I was always organically following what felt right and what showed up on my path. I know that it is precisely because I wasn't trying, that I've been able to develop it and be methodical about it. I have always observed and learned for a very long time before I saw patterns and accepted something metaphysical or spiritual as a truth. It has been a long, slow process of observing others and healing myself, along with risking following my intuition to new levels and growing from them.

The next mentor who showed up and shifted my world was Eric.

My transition to interior design didn't work out quite as I thought. In hindsight, it was mainly because I was distracted with Andy and the emergence of my spiritual path. So I decided to stop the program and work for a while. I had many typical part-time jobs—cashier jobs, work at restaurants, and a few months at a cosmetics company doing menial tasks and being utterly bored. One day, back in the first days of the 1-800 numbers for psychics, I saw an ad for people to give tarot readings for a new psychic hotline. I was terrified but I went to the interview anyway.

I arrived at the beautiful home of JZ Crystal, a psychic who had a little space above a restaurant in Montreal. She had invited thirty to forty psychics to join her and do phone readings. I did a fast three-card reading. She was clocking me to go fast and just say what I saw. Under pressure I had no time to filter what I would say, so it was nerve-wracking, but this is also how we grow to trust our intuition more. She said I read very well and hired me on the spot.

We worked in a rundown apartment full of phones, and it was very hard to concentrate. While we waited for it to get busy, we would exchange readings, and I met Eric. He was of European and indigenous descent, with a very strong sense of clairvoyance and a deep connection to his First Nations spirituality. He was the first to encourage me to say whatever I saw, even if it seemed crazy, I felt that openness and trust to be vulnerable, to describe the images or feelings I was receiving. It turned out that those things I would have kept to myself as "crazy" were almost always right. A whole new era began after that when I started to trust the full range of what I was receiving intuitively. After that, tarot became a tool to receive my clairvoyant messages; I would spread the cards, and the feelings and visions or messages would come.

It was a few more years of deep self-healing, which gave me even more self-trust and growth, before I began my career as a professional tarot reader, clairvoyant, and astrologer and could go out and help other people. I had a mission when I went back into Le Melange Magique years later to become one of their readers. It was based on my awareness that many people needed help to emancipate themselves from difficult circumstances and begin their healing journey. I felt compelled to help.

The journey of learning about multiple spiritual paths and traditions began at this store, as did my discovery that I was also clairaudient, clairsentient, and a medium. I had no idea until years of readings showed me patterns that I could name and draw from. Le Melange Magique was the departure point into my calling—a very deep dive into the psyche and the worlds of spirituality that brought me to where I am today. The store closed in 2013, one year after I left to work at the Westmount Wellness Center in Montreal, and I now have my own center in Sainte Anne de Bellevue, Quebec.

It's now my mission to help you take your intuition and self-trust to the next level—whatever you are comfortable with—so you can enjoy the magic, transformation, and healing of your higher guidance.

❧3❧

THE CLAIRS

T HE *CLAIRS* IS AN UMBRELLA TERM GIVEN TO what is called "clear abilities." It is understood in the definition that when this kind of intuitive information is received, it is pure, meaning it is not personal projection or a product of rational analysis. It is something that is clearly received with a particular sense. Once the vibration or information is received clearly, then we can begin to interpret what it may mean, but the original *clair* is something that just comes unbidden.

Clairvoyance is clear sight

Clairaudience is clear hearing

Clairsentience is clear feeling

Clairalience is clear smelling

Clairgustance is clear tasting

Clairtangency is psychometry, or knowing by touching an object

Claircognizance is clear knowing

You may have one or many or even all of these clairs at any given time. Some of us are more visual, and others of us are more emotional. Others get their guidance mainly in dreams. It truly doesn't matter which way you receive your intuitive guidance. What matters most is that you recognize the way it is speaking to you most, and then learn to discern the true message, as opposed to projecting the fears, fantasies, cravings, and aversions we all have. I'll help you do that!

Clairvoyance: Clear Seeing

Clairvoyance is likely our first association with psychic abilities, since we have seen it portrayed in movies and cartoons for generations. People have all kinds of assumptions about how clairvoyance works. We see it represented as if a full, detailed movie is played before our eyes with the exact timing, people involved, and meaning of the event, as if it's that cut and dried. The truth is that a lot of clairvoyance will be symbolic, not literal. This doesn't make it any less true or predictive, but it does make it harder to interpret.

True clairvoyance is a flash visual. That information can be a small instant flash, like a photo. That photo can be a small image—a shoe on the grass, a part of a desk with a paper on it, a person's face, or it can be a big image such as a house with land, the interior of a restaurant or club, or a full person who is cutting the lawn or dancing with your friend. The visual flash always has some truth to it if we don't start to project what it means and instead focus on what exactly was received.

When your vision is truly clairvoyant, it will come with no emotion attached to it.

If you have a flash of your ex-boyfriend talking to your friend and feel emotional about it right away, that is *not* clairvoyance. That is fear. If you have a flash of the ex-boyfriend talking to your friend and it comes like a brief flash photo, as if it walked across your brain and left, and there is no emotion attached to it, then it might be clairvoyant. We can't say 100 percent, though, unless you are over him fully and there is no possible way you are projecting a fear or fantasy about him talking to her.

In my experience, most of the time the clairvoyant information that turned out to be accurate had zero emotion and wasn't about people I had a strong attachment to. Sometimes it is so subtle you don't even realize it could be clairvoyance because there was no emotion. You don't react, so you might dismiss it!

Let me share a few examples of how it happens for me and others I know who are confident and accurate with their abilities.

Someone starts to talk about a person they just met and are interested in, and I get a flash of their face, body type, what they wear, and an overall feeling of their character. Most of the time this turns out to be accurate. Sometimes the age is off a bit but the other details fit—their character and even certain things they say or do. The initial clairvoyance is the flash visual of the person. The rest is part other clairs and also years of study. I know how certain people are once I see them.

Someone starts telling me about a house they want to sell, and I flash the interior or exterior of the house in some way and can describe it accurately and with details. Sometimes I know by the photo of a pet where everything is in that room or in the house—where the pet's room is in relation to the whole house, the lighting, air quality, and so on.

Someone talks about a business they want to start, and I flash the logo or one of their business partners' faces. From the visual information I then intuitively know other information about how the business will go.

It took years to develop to this degree of accuracy and interpretation. Let's look how it is more likely to happen when we're beginning:

1. You are starting to date again and wondering who you will end up with. As you are looking through the million and one profiles, you get a flash of a certain kind of car or shoes. You suddenly feel you *know* when you meet the right person that he or she will have this car or be wearing those shoes. If you are right, then this was clairvoyance. You foresaw an accurate detail that came true.

2. You want to rent a new apartment and are going through listings and driving around or walking to see places. When you pass one apartment listing, you have a flash vision of what the kitchen looks like. When you go see the space, you discover you were right. You got clairvoyant information.

3. You are having a birthday party soon and, as you are making the plans, you suddenly have a flash vision of a traffic jam. When natural clairvoyance is suppressed, it usually plays out like this: You start worrying for days leading up to the party that people will be late or some won't be able to come. You can't figure out why you are worrying so much but you can't stop. On the day of the party there is a traffic accident and a few of your guests are late. So you had the flash of the traffic jam and although you didn't know why traffic was bad, you were rightly worried people would be late. When you have more experience and trust your clairvoyance, you will know that a traffic jam is going to affect your party and you will probably make adjustments to the day or time or just your expectations.

In each case the visual flash came with no immediate emotion. If you can't shake the visual and start to have emotion afterward about what you see, that's a different story. The information was still clear of emotion when it was received. In the last example we see how it plays out after the vision is received. Usually it takes a bit of time and increased awareness to begin to see that we already have clairvoyant moments all the time in life. Many of them will be mundane and not change the course of our lives much. It is like the analogy at the beginning of this book about the hand. We don't wake up every day amazed that we have a hand that is doing all these things for us. Our awareness of our hand is there, but it isn't conscious and so it can slip under the radar unless we feel pain or pleasure. Clairvoyant information and flashes can also be like that. We hear so many things all day long on the news, or on social media, or crossing people's paths on the bus or street, and talking to friends or family. It would be quite overwhelming if we had to be fully conscious of every little thing we sensed from everyone all the time. We just could not process it.

So when a flash visual breaks through the psyche and catches your attention—it comes like a snapshot of something, a slice of life with no emotion attached to it—it may well be clairvoyant and accurate. When you have experiences like that, it's good to write down every detail that you can perceive without trying to figure out the meaning just yet. Simply describe everything you saw. It may be predictive!

Clairaudience: Clear Hearing

Things can become tricky with clairaudience because we associate hearing voices with mental illness, but many people hear things at some point in their lives. They hear a voice call their name. They hear a clear voice saying, "Don't go tonight," or "Take the bus," while they're considering driving or taking a train home. Other times it's a simple yes or no that comes when asking yourself something or hearing someone else ask for something. Here are some common ways clairaudience may first show up in your life.

1. You are at a party, and there is a gathering of people around you in the living room as you tell a story. You have everyone's attention as you tell people what happened and find yourself starting to say something insightful about it near the end. Everyone around you pauses for a

second and someone says, "Wow—pretty wise words there!" and you smile and feel a bit of a high, maybe laugh and say, "Yeah, no clue where that came from!" This happens all the time as we relax enough to let ourselves flow when talking. You will not be censoring yourself with self-consciousness or anxiety. You may be hearing your higher self—that wise part of you that knows. Other times you may be channeling a spirit around you without knowing it.

2. Someone tells you about a situation in which they need to make a decision about something complex or emotional. You listen to them tell the circumstances and weigh their options out loud and suddenly you hear a voice say, "Get a second opinion," or "Wait a month." It will be something that you suddenly hear that you feel compelled to say. It will be clear to you that you're receiving this message and have to say it right then and there. It won't be something you previously wanted to say as you were also weighing and analyzing their situation. It will pop out of nowhere and be very clear.

3. As you become more adept at listening to this inner voice or spirit guidance, you will start to hear more specific things. You may hear the name of a person or place. Sometimes you will hear a phrase rather than just a word, and it may have precise detail to it.

When clairaudience began for me, I had no idea it was happening, but I trusted what popped into my consciousness because it felt clear and true. I didn't question the source or even ask myself if this inner voice was my own higher self or a spirit guide. What I did notice was that, over the years of doing thousands of readings, I found myself saying more and more, "They are telling me . . ." and I would relay what I was hearing. Sometimes I heard words that I didn't know the meaning of in my waking life. I would hear legal jargon, technical terminology, names of cities I'd never heard of, and names sometimes. When I risked saying them—as I'd learned with my mentor Eric—even though it felt crazy (because I knew it wasn't coming from me) it almost always turned out to be relevant to the person sitting before me.

We all have an image of hearing voices in our head as if we are taken over, possessed by something evil we didn't invite and it now has control over our minds. This does exist, but it's also rare. It's important to be careful when we open up to clairaudience because—as I learned the hard way—the spirits that wish to speak through you aren't always good, and we have to learn to tell the difference. This is where mediumship begins—and that is beyond the scope of this book. If you're at a beginning level of clairaudience, you are safe to experiment and follow the words or phrases that pop up, but *only if* they don't suggest harming someone else or harming yourself. The same applies to clairvoyance. If you have a vision of harming another or self-harming—this is *not* clairvoyance and should never be acted upon.

A safe measure of when you can act upon the clairaudient messages you receive is this:

Positive guidance—your own or a spirit guide, angel, or ancestor—will always be simple, *non-directive* (not telling you what to do), giving a sense of relief or clarity. Anything you hear that brings stress, complicated thoughts or emotions, or bossy or directive energy is *not* clairaudience and should not be acted upon.

Your clairs should only bring you more clarity and ease in life.

Clairaudience when positive feels like a comforting voice, or a word that pops into your mind with no distress. It doesn't feel like something outside of you that wants to control you *at all*. When you tap into your true clairaudience, it can be a very helpful tool for life.

Clairsentience: Clear Feeling

To me clairsentience is just being a healthy human in some ways. We all feel things that other people are going through on some level. If someone is depressed and you spend time with them you will feel it too, or perhaps feel achy or tired afterward. This isn't to judge them, it's just the energy they have at the time, and we feel it and perceive it. If you identify as an empath, you have a higher degree of capacity to feel others' feelings, including physical feelings. Clairsentience occurs when you get a very strong and sudden emotion or physical sensation that you know is not yours. Once again it comes to you suddenly, strongly, and clearly. (Are you seeing the pattern here?) It is emotional and physical intuitive information that comes to you so quickly and without doubt that you usually feel compelled to share it right away. Here are some common ways clairsentience plays out in our lives:

1. A friend has had a breakup with a girlfriend or boyfriend and is quite upset. They reach out to you to talk or vent or cry, and you listen attentively and calmly. At some point in their story you get a sharp pain in your back. They feel relieved and you feel awful. You have absorbed or felt the deep fear, lack of support, or backstab they just received. Most of the time we end up thinking it is just us absorbing the sensation, even though it is painful. However, if we learn to ask ourselves, "Is this mine?" we can detach from it and often see that it had nothing to do with us. It was clairsentience giving us a message about the other person.

2. You are looking for a new home and are out at showings when you see a beautiful home and feel compelled to go inside. Once you start looking around at the perfect kitchen and beautiful moldings and windows you get an overwhelming sense that you want to cry. You don't understand what is happening because you have been in a great mood all day and really don't feel sad about anything in your life. You are very likely receiving clairsentience about that house or the people previously in it. You may inquire about the history of this house and discover there was a messy divorce or the loss of a parent recently and you felt the grief in the house.

3. You move into a new office within your company and are happy to be working in a bigger space with a better view and desk, but you notice you feel very tired in there and slowly find it harder to function, despite this improved space. You find out after a little research that the person who was there before you is on leave for depression and

anxiety. You felt the heavy energy and it played out as tiredness for you. It may also have turned into depression and anxiety for you as well, or headaches, insomnia, or any other symptom that tends to go with this condition. You may have had a harder time identifying this as clairsentience since we easily dismiss tiredness as a normal thing with change, stress, or not exercising. So the lesson here is to notice any shifts in your overall vitality and pinpoint when they started to see if you are feeling something that is not yours. There are many things to do to clear energy in a space once you have identified it as a problem.

One of the most unusual clairsentient moments I had in my career has always stuck with me. I had been doing readings at Le Melange Magique all day, and at the end of the day a woman walked in and within a minute of spreading the cards for her, I felt my hands go numb. I asked her if she had any pain or numbness in her hands and she said no. We spent a few minutes trying to figure out what this message was attempting to say and concluded it had to be symbolic. The numbness left when she did, and I was back to normal. It was definitely a message for her, but I never saw her again and don't know what happened to her, or if the symbolism ever made sense to her.

I will give you a couple of insights I learned over the years about strong physical sensations and what they tend to mean. The first one is sudden nausea or a sick-to-your-stomach feeling. This is a classic sign of abuse. This could mean you are being abused in the circumstance, or it could be the energy of a place, or person who is on some level abusing others. You may have this feeling while standing in a business that is a scam or a front. You may feel it around a perfectly charming person who is secretly aggressive to others. At any rate, in this instance it's not necessary to stay and figure out why—just leave and get yourself well again. You can decide what action, if any, to take later on if you feel the need.

The second one is when you feel sudden pressure or a lot of pain in the chest—as if someone landed a twenty-pound weight on your chest or something that is pulling or tugging your heart energy. This is a very uncomfortable sensation. If you can rule out that you have any heart problem yourself, it can be a sign of a narcissist or sociopath. Those sensitive enough will feel the imbalance and the absence of empathy in this way.

Finally, it's not all awful feelings, by the way! As you pass by people who are in love, you can also feel elated, a warm sensation, or tingling. You have access to your emotions to feel a full range, and that includes love, peace, and joy. If you are very clairsentient and empathic it will be really necessary for you to find environments, people, and self-care tools that support you and are a gentle refuge in life. It will also be necessary to learn how to cleanse your energy fields.

Clairalience: Clear Smelling

This is an interesting ability since smell has been proven to be our closest link to memory. It might be harder to discern when you are receiving a smell as a message, as opposed to your own memories or the presence of a spirit. Often people say they detect a whiff of roses or other flowers when the spirit of a loved one is around, or the person's perfume or cigar scent when their spirit visits.

I don't personally have clairalience, so I can't say much about its subtleties. However, I would imagine that we may receive any manner of smells as literal or symbolic intuitive messages. Perhaps someone is talking about going on a vacation and you suddenly smell salty air and find out they are visiting the ocean. You may wake up feeling stressed and smell something burning, and after checking that this isn't happening in your vicinity, you find out that there has been a fire in your city. You may have a memory of the particular burning smell and notice something chemical or gassy, to find out that it is a chemical or gas-based fire. You may be starting to date again, and as you look at online profiles you suddenly smell cologne or perfume, and a month or two later have a great date and suddenly remember that your date's cologne or perfume was the same one you smelled. These would be ways our clear smelling comes quickly and clearly as a message. Interpreting smell as a message may be a little tougher to have as a gift for other reasons as well. Smelling rotten eggs or cigarette smoke or chemicals and having to interpret them often would be unpleasant, to say the least.

Clairgustance: Clear Tasting

I hear far fewer examples of this one, but once in a while people will say they get tastes in their mouths that are messages. For example, someone might taste something metallic that lets them know that perhaps someone is ill, their water is contaminated, or the food they are eating was made with bad energy. It may be helpful with medical intuition to help diagnose.

We taste things all day as we eat our meals and snacks, so to have a sudden taste in your mouth at a time when you aren't eating or have just brushed your teeth or have a gum or mint in your mouth may also be tougher to spot or interpret. However, we say something "leaves a bad taste in our mouth" for a reason. It is associated with something morally wrong and suggests we can't digest or swallow someone else's words or behaviors. Whatever taste appears suddenly and clearly can be interpreted intuitively.

Clairtangency: Clear Touching of an Object (Psychometry)

Clairtangency, or psychometry, is an amazing ability because it not only gives you direct contact with the energy of its owner, but also where the object has been, information about the person wearing or holding it now, and sometimes the origins of who made the object. It also is an exciting clair because it helps verify that everything in the universe has a vibration and can be read or perceived. We touch an object and we get intuitive information from its vibration and make up.

According to professional musician Derek St. Holmes, who writes *The Invisible Universe* blog, "The Law of Vibration referenced from Bob Proctor, basically states that everything is in constant motion, which he generally referred to as vibration. There is no such thing as being at rest or motionless. According to the proposition of Proctor, everything even objects that everybody believes or considered as non-living things are actually moving. For example, a dining table, which appears to be motionless, is actually moving in ways not visible to the naked eyes. In his explanations, Proctor said that if they will use a microscope to view a certain portion of the table, they will see that millions of particles (commonly known as atoms) are in constant motion or vibration."

If you think of a piece of wood, something we consider very solid, as being at rest or static, then you don't expect it to change. It's as if it doesn't vibrate, so it should stay in the same condition. However it is just composed of a series of slower-moving particles, and over time the wood can dry out, warp, or twist, depending on the continued exposure to things like heat and moisture—even when the changes are very subtle.

I bring this up to illustrate that *all* things, no matter how solid they seem at first, are exposed to other elements and conditions, other vibrations, and can change. That includes the absorption of other energies such as emotion. This is why some things continue to work well for you and bring joy when you love them and they break or crack or don't work when you curse at them. Sometimes it is we who give the energy to the object and sometimes we're reading the energy of what has come before. I am sure if we wore the watch of a con artist, we would start to feel that trickster energy or find ourselves thinking about doing things we wouldn't otherwise have done.

Years ago I was working as a couturiere and costume designer. I was using industrial sewing machines and steam irons and over-lock machines every day that could be complicated, depending on the fabric involved. I was frustrated one night with my sewing machine, trying to get a piece done for a client, and called a friend to vent. I kept saying this "damned machine won't work properly tonight." She called me out on it, saying that if I stopped, calling it a "damned machine," it might work better for me.

From that day onward I decided to be conscious of my thoughts toward certain objects and do my best to send love or positive results to them. I started speaking nicely and visualizing positive results with my sewing machine after that, and it did function better! Still more proof that objects carry energy and absorb things just like we do. This is what can be perceived from psychometry. Let's look at some typical examples:

1. You are given your grandmother's ring, and when you wear it you dream of her, hear her voice, or have visions and memories of her. You may feel warmth, her touch, or other clairs activated by the ring.

2. You are shopping for used furniture and see a beat-up-looking old chair that looks *so* comfy. You sit down in it, and although its condition isn't the best, you decide to buy it because it gives you a strong feeling of home and safety.

3. You are shopping in a bookstore and pull a book off the shelf, and before you open the pages you get a strong vibe, vision, or emotion of

what this book is about and if it's for you. You randomly flip open to a page and read a phrase or two that fits your impression exactly.

I have had some very profound experiences with psychometry over the years. Most things I buy in a secondhand store are bought for the vibration they have. I've found great clothes that have feelings of self-care, self-discipline, organization, abundance, or wealth. And although lots of people are repulsed by the thought of wearing used clothing, preferring something new only, they are unaware that the new clothing still has a vibration on it from the seller, the store, and the designer and seamstress who made it.

Just because something is new doesn't mean the vibration is healthy. We can cleanse the object most of the time, but it's much harder with a house, larger object, or older object that has absorbed many things from many sources. For me, it's preferable to read and love the feeling of what you are buying or accepting as a gift on the spot. And we do this with psychometry. So all we need to do is hold the object, or sit on the furniture or in a car or house, and ask ourselves to allow the overall vibration and feeling of it to come to us, then trust the clairs to inform us intuitively.

I once read for a group of women who had moved to Montreal from Cambodia. They had hired me to give tarot readings, but one person asked me to hold her grandmother's pendant and tell her what I felt. I got such a strong and precise feeling of her grandmother that we were both in tears. The pendant was a very spiritual piece as well. Her grandmother was Buddhist and this pendant was probably fifty to sixty years old. I could feel not only her grandmother's personality and some events in her life, but I could also feel the spirituality or divine essence of the object that seemed to transcend her as a person. She had very strong faith and I could feel her connection to God or the divine through this pendant. It was truly beautiful and it was outside of my experience at the time. So I was able to perceive and feel a higher level of spiritual devotion and faith than I was conscious of currently in my own life. No wonder we were both crying!

After that, everyone in the party brought me rings, bracelets, and other pendants belonging to their mothers, grandmothers, and aunts all from Cambodia. The whole night was so beautiful, I never forgot it.

There is a sacredness in certain objects—jewelry, books, scriptures, old texts, churches, monasteries, homes, wells, tombstones, vases, fences, sculptures—*anything* can become sacred when the object is treated with love and reverence over time. When we give an object respect and care, it reflects it back to us and inspires us to continue to treat it as sacred. It's important that we all have something that is sacred to us. We can wear it or carry it, visit it, or have a photo or painting of it. It gives us a reminder of the sacred and divine in our lives and within ourselves and helps inspire hope and good behavior.

We practice a form of psychometry every day with our own closets, really. We are wearing clothing, belts, boots, coats, purses, briefcases, backpacks, and jewelry that all carry energy. You may have a shirt that still reminds you of good days in college. You may still be wearing something you wore to your previous job, and the one before that and the one before that, carrying this work identity with you from job to job. You might be wearing the wedding ring long after the divorce. We are all wearing energy every day and we can get so much intuitive information this way.

Psychometry is a common part of mediumship. Most people bring me the photos of lost loved ones, but many also bring me their objects. After jewelry, the most common thing people bring me is a piece of clothing to hold so I can more directly feel their loved one and connect to them on the other side.

What does this teach us? We need to be aware of the things we have around us and the energy they may carry that affects us. If you are living in the house where someone died with pain and difficulty and this home has not been cleansed by a professional—you are affected by this. You can mirror their pain or illness, or feel generally that life is not going well.

People often call it bad luck, but it's deeper than that. If you are living in the home where a beloved but happy person died, you may still feel them around in a good way—feeling secure or supported. As long as you aren't grieving and longing for this person too often, it's a good experience. If you wear the jewelry of someone you loved, the same thing applies. It can bring you their energy, overall outlook on life, and health issues, or their patterns can emerge if you wear it all the time. If you still have something around from an ex and wonder why you can't move on or meet someone else, it's time for it to go.

Objects can bind us to people, times, and places as well. The story, emotions, and events that an object carries can be transmitted to you if you inhabit, wear, or use it often. Pay attention to your thoughts, feelings, and vitality level regarding different objects in your life. If you detect that you feel heaviness, sadness, anxiety, or anger when using or wearing something, you can try to cleanse it first with sage-smudging and prayer. If it doesn't clear up and give you a good feeling of lightness or support, then it's time to discard it. And just the same, if something you use, inhabit, or wear gives you positive feelings and harmony, you can keep sending love and gratitude for it and it can gradually become sacred for you.

Claircognizance: Clear Knowing

Clear knowing is probably the most common experience of intuition and is frequently the first sense that comes to you before the other clairs. Most people have at least some experiences where they can say they just "know" something. They have no clue how they know, by what senses the intuition came to them, but they know that they know.

Most people I have met who have strong claircognizance are also totally comfortable to leave it at that. They don't seem interested to discover the source of their knowing. Someone of this type could be described as a very pure and honest intuitive person in the sense that they have a full trust of their inner knowing and they usually act on it. Most people tend to start analyzing or wondering why or what things mean and can miss the window to act on that sudden knowing. They get caught up in the analytical mind, where there often aren't answers or closure. People who are strongly claircognizant tend to live by it and aren't big analyzers.

It's a shame, really, because their gift is very strong and could be turned into any of the other clairs if they were to develop it. When I do intuition trainings, I gently push the person who says, "I just *knew*." When they are accurate about a question someone posed, I get them to close their eyes and bring to mind the sensation they had when they knew. Once they have been able to locate this sensation, I ask them if they saw an image, if they heard a word, if they feel any bodily sensation or strong sudden emotion. Ninety-nine percent of them end up identifying another clair that came to them as they just *knew* something. I consider claircognizance to be the gateway to realizing you already have other strong clair abilities. Let's look at some common ways claircognizance plays out in daily life:

1. You get up in the morning and as you are making your coffee, you have a strong sudden knowing that the highway you take to work is closed, so you automatically and without question or checking the news first decide to take another route.

2. You realize that you lost an object somewhere during the day, and you know where it is (and turn out to be right).

3. You are involved in planning something that requires certain steps and logistics, and along the way to making decisions about the order of operations, you just *know* a bunch of things that will happen—and suggest the solution. This could be a knowing that there will be delays with something, that someone's design has a flaw, that something will take longer in reality than the projected time, and so on. When you propose your solution, it will be as if you jumped over all these steps simultaneously and that solution will seem clear and obvious—to you. Often people around you will be lost or won't agree, and it may be hard for you to explain how you know what you know!

As you can well imagine, there are frustrations for a claircognizant person because you suddenly know, but you often can't tell people why or how you know. If you are aware of your other clairvoyant abilities or clairaudient abilities, it can make it a bit easier to explain to people.

You can say, "I had a flash of that floor plan not working in that corner." You can say, "I don't know, but when he described losing his watch I suddenly heard 'stairwell.'" You at least have a clear intuition and information to start a conversation with.

When it is, "I don't know; I just *know*," people really can't say anything to that and are often left in the dark in some way, and you may be quite frustrated if people don't take your suggestions seriously. It is well worth developing your gifts more to see which of the clairs is strongest in you, so you can communicate the valuable intuitive information to others.

I had a lot of claircognizance as a child and into my teens before I could articulate what was going on and why my knowing was right. I always *knew* when people weren't happy, when they were hiding their true feelings, and what those true feelings were—even though most would never admit to having them.

One of the stronger examples I have of claircognizance was during my arrival in Montreal and my application to Dawson College. I applied for interior design school and came to visit Montreal twice looking for apartments before I found the right one. One day a letter came from Dawson College and I realized, "Oh my God, I moved here before I even knew for sure I got into the program!" But I just *knew* I would—to the point that I moved three hours away to a different culture.

I *love* when the moments of knowing come that strongly. It's rare when they come to us about very important steps and decisions that affect our future. Many people describe knowing that their spouse would be their husband or wife when they first met or very early on. Lots of people will describe just knowing that they were going to live or move somewhere after only visiting or seeing a place.

We all get those strong feelings in life at some point. There is nothing more wonderful than a strong knowing surrounding a life decision or positive event. You know your daughter is having twins, and she does. You know someone likes you, and the relationship unfolds. You know your project or book will succeed, and it manifests easily. It feels magical to be that aligned.

We also know when there are painful events too—not fun to live, but we can often be way ahead of the game and be more effective dealing with them. We know that someone is not coming home from the hospital this time, so now we can prepare for what's next instead of being in denial and usually bringing on more stress or crisis. We know that our sudden ache or pain is more serious, so we go to the doctor right away. We know that a couple isn't compatible and won't last, so we can be sensitive and helpful or supportive of that transition. It's endless the things you will just know that you can act upon.

The more you are aware and honor those times of knowing, the more you will see that they are usually accurate and can act on them safely. It's hard to truly describe how much is going on in, on, and around us at any given time that can't be quantified or analyzed quickly. But it *can* be felt or intuited quickly and can help you and even save your life sometimes.

There is a vibration to everything in the universe. You can develop your senses to the point where you recognize certain vibrational patterns and know with confidence what they are. In every profession and field where someone has mastered a skill or a body of knowledge, there are very precise sensations or qualities—vibrations—this expert recognizes and can respond to.

An oncologist knows subtle signs of cancer, remission, and severity. A musician knows notes, timing, and chord structure and therefore has a more refined sense of playing with them to create effects—that is, arranging music to create an intended mood.

Mastery of different elements and tools, psychological and physical states, animal or plant behavior—it is an infinite and endless amount of vibrational information in the universe to read. Mediums have learned to master other realms of sensation and pattern as well.

A police officer or investigator can spot a thief and a liar faster than most untrained people can. People who have mastered something will have that sixth sense about their area of expertise. For psychics and mediums, intuitive development *is* the sixth sense we master.

⭐4⭐

TRUE INTUITION VERSUS FEAR, PROJECTION, IMAGINATION, OR DESIRE

THIS IS THE TRICKY PART! HOW DO WE KNOW WHEN our intuition is real or just our imagination, fear, desire, or projection? This might be the most asked question I get when people open up to their gifts. There is a very real fear of trusting ourselves, and I would dig even deeper to say there is a very real fear of delusion or insanity that operates under this question. We want to believe in the mystical but we are afraid of fooling ourselves or being fooled. We long to relax into acceptance with our higher self and the insights we receive via intuition, but we are terrified that we might be making it all up and will lead ourselves astray—and be judged as crazy.

These fears were very real to me as well, having grown up in the shadow of my aunt's bipolar disorder and the fear of emotion in general that went unexpressed a lot of the time in my family, and the culture of hiding what we truly felt and knew. I was terrified of being sent to a psychiatrist for saying I was studying astrology—let alone when I began to study the tarot and, heaven forbid, when I came into my path of clairvoyance, channeling, and mediumship. All this is to say I took my own process of believing my own abilities *very* slowly and almost scientifically.

I began to read and study astrology at around age fifteen in the shopping mall bookstores when no one was around. I found myself terrified to even pick up the books, yet I was compelled, and over time I resonated with astrology more and more. I started to figure out people's signs and started by observing my family to see if the descriptions seemed true or not, and they were. I expanded it maybe two years later to friends and continued to observe. I hadn't knowingly met people of every sign, so I left my conclusions open until many years had gone by and I'd had personal experience with all the signs, and still I learn today after thirty-five years of observations. I was always good with patterns. I could see them visually in my designing and sewing, and I could see them in people too. My journey to being able to say what I believe to be true—whether it is about an astrology aspect, a tarot card, intuition, or clairvoyance— has been very slow and has included years of self-observation with a healthy skepticism. Many things I now believe I also thought were crazy at first, given the academic family I grew up in. I am grateful for this background now, because it gave me the solid anchor from which to observe and open up to the metaphysical realm. What I have come to know in the patterns of intuition and the clairs, when they are real and not self-generated, has also been through years of observation and testing with thousands of readings in which many people have given validation.

REAL OR TRUE INTUITION

When intuition is true or real or accurate, there are certain characteristics of the experience. First of all, the information comes to you through one of the clairs and is sudden. It doesn't usually come reliably and accurately while pondering, worrying, or analyzing something or someone. It usually comes when you are in the middle of doing something else, and it hits you. In your mind, you see someone you know and haven't seen for ages, and then days later you see them or hear news about them. You might have been doing the dishes when they entered your mind for a millisecond. So the suddenness and the randomness is part of it when it is real.

The second part that is so important is that intuitive information that turns out to be accurate comes to us with no emotion attached to it. I was lying in bed one night a few years ago, eyes closed and about to fall asleep with my cat, when I had a flash of my uncle at his cottage falling off a ladder and dying. I hadn't talked to him in years and wasn't worrying about him at all at the time. He wasn't on my mind in the least when this happened. During the flash I felt no emotion. I was shown a little movie clip. Afterward the ethical questions started—whether to tell or not. A few weeks later I heard that my second cousin had fallen off a ladder and had had a stroke and died. He was of similar age and height and was balding like my uncle, and his cottage was right beside my uncle's cottage. I was sad to hear of his passing, but I knew I had been shown that moment for a reason and couldn't have prevented it. My emotions came after the vision, not before or during.

Usually, the visions are very mundane, not life-altering. They are about ordinary events and come as a flash or a word and without any emotion, so they are often dismissed or missed entirely. Perhaps you are wondering when your wife will be home from work and flash a construction sign. If you are not feeling any emotion with the image and you sense that she may be late due to construction on the roads, then you may have experienced real or true intuition—clairvoyance. Often things like this go under our radar since we can easily justify construction with logic, and being late home isn't unusual. Perhaps instead you flashed the image of a computer and felt she had to stay late because there was more work or her computer was slow. Again it's a mundane example, but it is still specific enough. And if you turned out to be right, it counts!

The emotion surrounding your intuition or vision tends to come later, once you process what you saw. Let's say your niece is dating someone new, and you know how badly she wants to get married. You ask her what the new boyfriend's name is. As soon as you hear the name, you also hear "Nope" or "It's not him." Now what? Your emotions aren't involved, but hers are and you care about her. You had no previous knowledge of this man or anything to have an opinion before you asked her—and the words just hit you quickly and loudly.

This is clairaudience in action. Only time will tell if you are right in this case, and you have a decision to make about telling her your intuition or not. You can just be aware and be ready to support her along the way if she becomes unhappy down the road.

Quick and clear sensations, knowing, words, or flash visions with no emotion are often real and accurate. We still need to be cautious though. We need to observe these flashes and intuitions for a while to make sure that our sense is accurate and see patterns in them before we can start telling people anything that may alter their lives. Clairaudience comes with responsibility.

FEAR

Fear is a totally different vibration from insight. When we are in fear, our minds are not calm. We have a racing heart and racing thoughts that go in circles. We often have worst-case scenarios playing in our heads that are mostly *not* going to happen. When we are in fear, we can't hear our intuition. We are in fight or flight and we will be strongly compelled to act for survival. This isn't intuition.

Fear is an imbalance of the mind. Intuition arrives when the mind is very calm. When you are fearful and worried and then see an image of someone or something happening, 99 percent of the time you are imagining worst-case scenarios instead of seeing true outcomes. It can be very hard to peel ourselves away from the spiral of fear and worst-case scenarios at times. Let's look at how fear may disguise itself as intuition:

1. You are in love, and the man of your dreams hasn't called or texted in the last twenty-four hours. You start to worry. Maybe something happened to him and he is late or tired today. You start running through every possibility for why he hasn't called today, when you get a flash of him with another woman. You become extremely sad or angry and can't calm down. You start getting a visual of his ex-girlfriend or a woman you think is his ideal woman. You have worked yourself into a state of panic and perceived rejection. Just when you are sure he is cheating on you because of this vision, he calls you and apologizes for being late and says he can't wait to see you.

2. You are going on a vacation soon and are looking forward to the beach, but you are always a little nervous about flying. You are doing your best to stay calm, but one night before you leave you wake up with a dream of a plane crash. You start to fear that your plane will crash or something awful will ruin your trip. You can't stop thinking about getting on the plane and finding an awful person sitting next to you, or security not letting you on the plane, or food poisoning. All your fears are coming up and you feel sure something bad will manifest. You are considering canceling your trip. You decide to go anyway, despite the fear as you board, because you paid for the trip and you might be wrong, and you have a great flight and a nice trip. Your fear did not manifest in any way, so your visions were not intuition.

3. You are told you need a small surgery to remove a cyst and are feeling anxious about it. All kinds of fears and flashes come to your mind.

They are vivid images, so are they real? Maybe you see yourself having complications during the surgery, or they find cancer somewhere else once they open you up, or the anesthesia doesn't work and you're awake during the operation—all kinds of scenarios play out in fear. You have your cyst removed, and everything is smooth sailing and you are treated well at the hospital, and feel great afterward. So what happened? Why all the visions? It's pure fear—possibly stemming from a previous circumstance or someone else who is close to you. It could be related to a past life, and, of course, worst-case scenarios can be a way to cope with the unknown.

Let's take a look at how these same situations would be different when the intuition is real.

1. So, you are in love and your partner hasn't called or texted in the last twenty-four hours. No problem. You trust him and know you will hear from him. Your connection is very strong and you feel no worry. The next morning you wake up feeling fine, looking forward to hearing from him when he can contact you, and you go about your day. You go to work, stop at the grocery store, and are on your way up the stairs to your front door when you feel nauseated. You see his face in your mind and know something is off without knowing what. You have an overwhelming and repetitive thought, "We have to talk," that hits you right after. The absence of a call or text on top of your sudden nausea and "We have to talk" message can mean many things, so when you see him next you gently ask if he was having a horrible day or if he was dealing with someone toxic in his life around

that time, and you gauge if he is withholding from you or the love vibration is broken before questioning his fidelity. And even if you do question him, you can phrase it as your fear and see where the conversation goes, trusting your intuition during that conversation as well. Cheating is such an easy thing to jump to, and unfounded accusations destroy trust, so it's important to be very sure and speak carefully. However, nausea is a common clairsentient example of a toxic relationship, a breach of trust or morals, or of abuse. So it should be heeded and followed up on.

2. The vacation. The hotel is booked, you have your plane tickets and everything you need, and you have been truly excited about your trip for weeks without a worry. You hail a taxi and are off to the airport. As you are waiting in line for your boarding pass, you get a sudden feeling of claustrophobia that isn't common for you. You suddenly feel it's a bit hard to breathe. You start to suddenly become very worried about where your seat will be on the plane, so you ask to have your seat switched. The flash feeling leaves your body as you switch seats and the claustrophobic feeling is now gone. You glance at who you would have been sitting next to before the switch and it all becomes clear to you that this person would have triggered discomfort. So in this case you have fear, but a very specific fear. It came quickly, but because you acted on it quickly, it left. You can trust that it was either clairsentience or claircognizance, and you averted discomfort.

3. You get your ultrasound, and the doctor tells you that you have a small benign cyst on your neck and it's best to remove it so no other

problems arise down the road. You feel very reassured that your doctor is taking care of you and have no fear of the actual surgery. The night before you go into surgery, you have a dream that there is a dark circle around the cyst in your neck. You wake up in the morning curious about this dream and wonder if they will find something else when they remove it. In the dream the dark circle was completely removed, so you are more curious than scared. Right before they prep you for surgery, the doctor comes to tell you that they have looked at the ultrasound one more time and there may be more to remove than they thought, and you may feel a bit scared, but you trust that in your dream the dark circle (the cyst) is all removed, and you know you will be fine. After the surgery the doctor tells you they removed a slightly larger area than they thought but it is all clean now.

I had a sensation in my right breast six years ago and kept worrying I might have something wrong, so I went to my doctor and gynecologist, and both said I was fine. I was a bit puzzled because I did feel a sensation like a lump. A few weeks later my mom was diagnosed with breast cancer in the right breast, right where I'd felt it. This is clairsentience and empathy. She waited for her surgery, and the morning it happened I literally felt it gone in my breast— the sensation wasn't there, and the breast felt clean. I called her and said, "The surgery is clean, Mom. No more cancer." And she has been clean and clear for five years. This was intuition because I didn't panic. I felt something strongly enough to investigate it, and it turned out to be not mine and then my sensation was correct about her surgery. I didn't get emotional at any point in this chain of events, so I knew it wasn't fear. I realize it can be very hard to tell this difference when fear overtakes you. So if you follow the basic principles that true intuition that is predictive does not come when in fear—you can coach yourself to look at where the fear *is* coming from and not place it on your current situation.

PROJECTION

It took me a long time in life to understand projection well and to be able to spot it when I was doing it to others and when people were projecting onto me. We have to really know ourselves well before we can spot what is our baggage versus someone else's. If you grew up in a home with weak boundaries, this may be hard to grasp at first. You will be used to everyone blaming or putting their fears, emotions, thoughts, and outcomes onto you, and you likely became codependent and did it in return. After a long journey of healing you will be able to feel yourself as an independent person and be able to own your good traits as well as your shadow traits, and no one will be able to gaslight you and alter your self-perception. You will also be fully responsible for your own life and not put it on others. Seeing through projection takes maturity. Let's look at how projection can seem like intuition:

1. Let's return to the example of cheating. A classic example of projection would be a cheating man or woman who accuses their partner of cheating. They can't admit to themselves or their partner that they

are cheating, so they blame the other person for being deceptive in some other way, or say they can't trust them, when it is they who can't be trusted. If we look at how projection could be misinterpreted as intuition in this case, we would see the cheater having a flash vision of the faithful partner hiding something from them. The cheating person may have a sudden feeling that their partner withheld money from their last paycheck. They check their bank accounts and, sure enough, there is money missing. They feel sure the partner didn't tell them they bought something or had a smaller pay than usual. After fighting about this, the partner checks the bank account and sees a purchase for a hotel room, and the secret is out. The cheater was right about missing money but was so busy projecting onto the partner that he missed that it was his own illicit purchase. Projection is a very slippery slope. If you are trying to hide anything from others or yourself, your intuition will probably not be reliable, and you may do a lot of projecting and accusing in the name of having a feeling or vision.

2. Another common projection occurs when someone in your life parallels the look or personality traits of someone who hurt you in the past. It can be very difficult to separate the present person from the person they remind you of. An example of confusing projection and intuition in this case could be quite hard to spot. You meet someone and are instantly attracted. Everything is going well on your first few dates and you are feeling closer and hopeful. You are getting ready for a nice dinner out when you get an overwhelming feeling of rejection. You suddenly feel sure this person is going to reject you for your appearance.

Your hair is wrong, your nose is too big, you are too fat, and so on. You go out to dinner and are happy to be there but you're also agitated, anticipating that the gut feeling you had will play out. He asks you if you want more dessert, and you lose it, telling him, "I knew you were going to reject me." He hasn't said or done anything to even hint at that. You have a good long heart-to-heart about what happened and realize that, years ago just as you were falling in love, someone who was scared to go farther blamed your appearance as his reason to break up. You maybe haven't fully processed or grieved this relationship, so you projected it onto this new person who gave no indications of rejection. So your gut feeling in this case was deeply buried trauma that came out. This is so common, and it breaks my heart every time I see it. People so often cannot see that their fear-based gut feelings or visions are unprocessed trauma. It's very hard to see it in ourselves without help from a good therapist or friend or a very understanding partner!

3. Another common projection that causes us trouble but seems positive at first comes when we project good traits or abilities on to people who don't possess them. You meet someone new, and there is that strong attraction. You know they are attracted and you start to feel special or sexy. You start to be more open and flirty with them, letting down your guard and talking more about your life. Everything is feeling wonderful with all the adoration you are enjoying. You get a strong vision of this person in your home, cuddling with you and your dog. The vision is so clear that you feel sure this person is the *one*. You start dating and find that they say and do things that do not match up with your vision or with what they say. Your vision was so strong, so you believe it

must have been real. But as the months go by, you feel less special, less connected, and your partner has become more controlling. You can't figure out what happened because your feeling of love and your vision were so strong at first. In this case, you have probably been bitten by a narcissist! You were projecting all your healthy and loving traits on to this emotionally bankrupt person. This is a common projection and a very painful one. If you are really honest with yourself, you *did* have true intuitions about the person all along, but you were likely drunk on their attraction, and vulnerable to needing their attention. Go back and be honest with yourself what the red flags were. They are always there, and that vibration is the voice of intuition. That first incongruence of loving behavior you felt—that was it.

FANTASY AND IMAGINATION

People often ask, "How do I know I am not just making it up because I want that to happen?" We so often don't trust good information when it comes through. We are inclined to fear the bad and take it seriously, and the wonderful outcomes we reject and say we must be fantasizing. This is precisely why we all need to know what true intuition is, so when information is scary or life altering, we act on it instead of worrying and waiting. And then to trust it when it is good and allow hope and joy into life.

Fantasizing is another vibration we can learn to spot. Visualizing what we want is useful and can help us focus on what we want. When we become good at visualizing, it tends to manifest. We allow the vision into our psyche as a focusing tool, trying it on for size and adjusting to the feeling of having a great relationship, job, or home. When we fantasize, we start to be ungrounded. There is a floating feeling—a high—and a lot of idealizing. It feels great—at first. Fantasy can be the beginning of manifesting or the rabbit hole of addiction. In a fantasy, everything is smooth and perfect and easy—including people. That's where it can all go south.

In fantasy, we spend a lot of time building a vision that we desire, lingering over every detail of how and when and what it all looks like ideally. We can become so attached that we reject good opportunities because they don't match the fantasy. Use the initial desire and fantasy to get in touch with very deep and important values, and then allow things to manifest as they are. Fantasy can be rigid; it does not allow anything in and is isolating. Visualization, to manifest something you want, has a more dynamic energy. It isn't rigid in the how or the who—it opens life up to intuition and more self-trust.

Let's look at how fantasy is confused as intuition: Let's say you are single and want a relationship very badly. You have been listening to all kinds of videos and programs to manifest your soulmate. You write down traits and qualities you want the person to have. Your list has a detailed description of physical appearance, activities you will do together, values you share, careers, and even where you would live. It's built into your ideal person. As you are envisioning this person, you get a flash of someone with very dark, beautiful hair and feel sure that your soulmate will have this gorgeous hair you see. You are at a conference and connect with someone during one of your seminars. You run into him at lunch and during the second half of your conference. You have a lot in common and there is a spark—but he is blond. So you don't pursue this connection. By fixating on insignificant details, like hair color, eye color, or height, you completely miss the whole person! You may see or hear something very strong when fantasizing—so strong you feel it is a sign—and then miss the opportunity in front of you.

In a fantasy there is very strong attachment. We *must* find someone with dark hair, or we *have* to live in that neighborhood (even if all other things match and it's two miles away). We can't trust the visions we get or the message we hear when we are fixated and attached to a certain outcome. We simply aren't open to anything *but* our fantasy. Another big clue is our reaction to the flash or message. When we are fantasizing, we will be disappointed or high right after, not in an open or impartial state. We can only trust what comes in a calm, detached state, without a big reaction either way when it happens.

When we are in the state of manifestation, it is another vibration altogether. We have a list of qualities of our soulmate, but it's less likely to be itemized about height, hair color, profession, and so on. It is usually based on the overall quality of connection, the interests and values you share. This person may be different from our mental image, but we have affirmed that we want a strong attraction, so it will be there. It may just be in a different package from what we thought. In manifestation we recognize connection and energy. It's not a checklist. This is one huge difference between manifestation and fantasy.

＊5＊

HOW DO I DEVELOP MY ABILITIES?

ANYONE CAN DEVELOP STRONGER INTUITION skills. It's like singing—we can all sing. Some of us have a talent for it and it comes more easily, but if we rehearse and learn to breathe better and allow blocked emotions to flow, we will sing better. Intuition is similar. There are certain kinds of activities that help open it up, and certain conditions in life that help us act on it. And similar to singing, intuition requires the throat and heart to be so open that the emotions can flow as a beautiful song. The body lets go to vibrate and be a conduit of the sound. With intuition we must both learn to allow a flow of energy and information to come through us and learn to discern.

It takes a calm mind to receive intuition. How many of us have a calm mind? Not many these days. We have chronic anxiety in our society, so our minds are spinning and running and worrying or addicted to something to keep us high. Many of us struggle with depression, apathy, feeling numb, or not being very hopeful. All states of suffering make it very hard to hear or see or feel in a clear manner. This is why, for many of us, intuition will come in a breakthrough moment. We are doing something calm or repetitive and get insight. We are exercising or doing yoga and we get a flash. It comes before bed as we are calmer, or upon waking. Some people get only a few strong intuitions in a lifetime and these tend to occur around big life events such as a birth, death, or wedding.

If we want to increase our ability and hear our intuitive guidance more, we must learn to calm the mind. This is a bigger task than we may think! In 2002 I went to a Vipassana meditation retreat. It was ten days of silence with nothing but myself to sit with. The purpose was to confront our sensations and train the mind. It was a profound experience and it wasn't easy. The teacher said over and over that it takes three days of sitting in meditation for the mind to calm down. Three days! We are lucky if we can sit for ten minutes and calm down. The three-day mark was a very hard day at the retreat. People were ill, crying, or fidgety. I had a huge flashback of a childhood memory and a lightning bolt of energy that sent me down the hall crying. We all carry so much unprocessed emotion and experience that it takes days (if not a lifetime) to digest. Our minds are rarely calm unless or until we develop practices to ground and calm the body and mind regularly. Even then, life still happens! Let's look at some important aspects to developing your clair abilities:

1. **MEDITATION.** Any type of meditation will help calm you on some level and help your whole system relax, and with that, you will start to process your life. As you sit and breathe in meditation for longer periods, discomfort rises and passes, and anger flares up and passes. It takes time initially to calm the waves of emotion and anxiety, but it is worth it. Deeper levels of meditation open you to insight and intuition. As your body is calmer and your mind more relaxed, you start to remember the subtle details of your life. Meditating sometimes brings you intuition while you just sit. You are focused on your technique, contemplation, guided relaxation, breath, or mandala—but suddenly there may be a flash visual or the sound of words, a sudden strong claircognizance. Learn how to calm your mind to open yourself more deeply to allow these experiences to happen.

2. **OBSERVATION.** Meditation we do in our own space, inner sanctum, or cocoon to let us relax and delve into our inner being. Observation is more of a waking meditative state. If you hang back from sharing and feeling pressure to keep up with conversations or story lines, you will observe what is between the lines. When you release your attachment to being heard or participating, you can feel the pulse of the situation. You may gain insight into people you have known for years by observing, without judgment, what they are doing, saying, how they move, what patterns you see. Once you have moved into an observer stance, you may find that your intuition is heightened and may get clairvoyant or clairsentient information. The beauty of this is that if you maintain the observer role, you can then verify if what you saw or heard or felt plays

out. When I began to study astrology, the first several years were for studying and observing patterns before saying anything to anyone. Keep what you see to yourself and notice when your intuitions turn out to be true. You have to go within to hear what is within. Competing to be heard or to be taken seriously takes enormous energy and detracts from going within for inner guidance.

3. **JOURNALING.** We have to keep track of our growth as we develop our abilities or we run the risk of slipping into fear, projection, and fantasy. Journaling is also an excellent way to process daily life. We take in so much energy all day from media and coworkers, the cities we live in, and other people's problems. Where does it all go? If we don't process it and filter it well, it bottlenecks and gets stuck. To hear the flow of our intuition we have to be able to release what builds up inside so there is room to receive. Keeping a journal is also a great way to track your progress. You can begin by writing your first impressions of anything—a new person you meet, a new place you ate at, a breaking news story. Write down what you feel before anything skews your first impression. Keep doing this, along with noting any other flashes or observations you have, and gradually you will see when you are right. Over time you will see that when you received a true clairvoyant flash, an accurate message, or a dream about something, it had a specific sensation when it came to you.

4. **PATTERNS.** When we deeply observe ourselves, our own process, and events or people around us, we will see patterns. Identifying patterns takes our awareness up to the next level. When you spot a pattern and

you feel confident of it, now you can catch yourself in it, or see when others are in theirs—and the next layer of observation and insight begins. It's an ever-unfolding onion of awareness.

5. **PERMISSION TO BE RIGHT.** People can stay stuck wondering and analyzing what their intuition could mean, or if it's real or not real. Once you have calmed your mind and have begun to observe more, it's time to get curious and test yourself. Instead of having your mind on the hamster wheel, I want you to think, "If I am right, then what?" This takes you to the next level. For example, you meet someone new, and the interaction is awkward. You don't know this person and worry, "Am I judging them? What if I'm the awkward one, and they are mirroring me?" You can go on and on with no resolution. The only thing you can rely on is your intuition about the brief interaction. So ask yourself, "Am I anxious or awkward normally?" If not, then it isn't yours. "Did I just have an uncomfortable or awkward interaction with someone else, and it's still in my energy field?" If yes, then ask yourself if there is any parallel between the people involved. If no, then again, it's not yours. "Am I judging them?" No. You are receiving a vibe and trying to understand what to do with it. You aren't condemning anyone as a bad person. They may not be awkward every day! Finally I would say, "What if I am 100 percent right in everything I sense about this person? What else do I now sense is true?" Stay open to anything that now comes to you. Write it in your journal. Developing your abilities is a process and needs space and patience.

❋6❋

INTUITION IN ACTION

INTUITION IS A SPECTRUM, LIKE MANY THINGS IN life. We all have it, but some of us are not aware that we are acting on it, while others experience it daily and aren't sure what to do with it! Intuition runs the gamut, from mundane things that you sensed or knew that don't alter your life to intuitions that are so precise and detailed that they are predictive and inform your life choices. Let's look at this spectrum in a progression and see where you fit.

- ❀ You are driving to work and get a feeling about taking a different route. You find out later that you avoided an accident.

- ❀ You are at a restaurant and want to order something you love; but for some reason feel it's a *no* to order it, so you choose something else. You later find out you were allergic to something in that recipe. You dodged a bad stomach.

❀ Your son is acting up again and your partner wants to be firmer about his punishment, but you feel he just needs a day home from school. You tell your partner and let your son stay home. You have one of the best days you've had with him in a long time and at the end of it he tells you he is being bullied at school.

❀ You are crunched for time to study for your final exam and there is no way you can read everything required. You look at your course materials and intuit which chapters are most important. You turn out to be right and pass with flying colors.

❀ You are lost on vacation in an unfamiliar place. You scan the people and businesses quickly and trust the vibe of everyone you see, choosing someone who feels safe and friendly. You ask for help, and they walk you to your destination.

❀ You meet someone online and they want to meet you for a date. They ask you for coffee and you suddenly flash a vision of your local café. You decide to have them meet you in a place you already know, where you feel safe.

❀ You get a call from a potential client and, by their voice, you get a strong feeling of what this person looks like or act like. When you meet them, you have proof that you were right.

❀ It is your birthday, and you have family and friends gathered for dinner. Someone passes you a gift and, as you touch it, you get a strong vision of what is inside. You describe the gift in detail and turn out to be correct.

- ❈ You see a notification on social media that someone you know but haven't seen since college is "in a relationship." You hear wedding bells when you look at the photo. A few months later the couple announces their wedding engagement.

- ❈ Your grandma tells you she is going to the doctor for routine tests and you get a sharp pain in your abdomen on the right. You know this is her pain, not yours, and you suspect issues with her digestive system. She is diagnosed with a liver issue.

- ❈ Your sister calls you, as she does every week, but this time when you pick up the phone, you see pink everywhere around her. She tells you she is pregnant with a baby girl.

Examples are endless, aren't they? It's always something you see, hear, or feel physically or emotionally that comes effortlessly, clearly, and with detachment. When you pay attention to it, take it seriously, and act on it, there will be many wonderful moments, as well as some tough things that perhaps can be avoided or prevented. The stronger your ability to receive, the more precise your intuitions will be, and they become more and more accurate and predictive.

After the Twin Towers fell on September 11, 2001, I asked a few fellow mediums if they had had a sign or signal about the terrorist attacks and, if so, how the messages came. The one that struck me most was colleague and medium Valerie, who said the night before it happened she had dreams of running down staircases and fire all night long. She was tapping into the people in the towers and their experience. For me it was about three weeks before that I received a sign but, honestly, I had no idea it would be a terrorist attack. Being North American before that awful day meant I grew up sheltered from even thinking it could happen here. I was watching TV in my living room and sewing by hand—as I did often. One of my favorite shows came on, *The Sopranos*, and I was still looking at my sewing as the theme song started. At one point I stopped dead, looked up, and looked for the Twin Towers in the skyline. I thought to myself, *OK—still there*. I truly had no idea this meant something was going to happen to them. My life had become so full of moments like that, so I was used to having flashes but also waiting to see how things played out.

As I write this book, we are waiting and wondering if our town is going to flood again this year. We had it very bad in 2017 in the Montreal area, and my neighbors had to be evacuated. It took months to clean and rebuild their homes, so we have all been sensitized to the water levels since then and are very cautious. As my whole town is making preparations once again, I know it won't be as bad as that last time was. How do I know? I felt it months ago and wasn't worried. I asked others if they felt worried this year, and everyone said no. We often get a collective vibe on things if we think to ask and see patterns. We also just had a restaurant burn down, and everyone was upset, but within twenty-four hours, at least three local people mentioned to me they wondered if there was something corrupt going on. When I saw the fire with my own eyes, within an hour or so I also kept hearing "insurance" over and over. Now the latest news is that there was a grow-op upstairs that's under investigation. So again, collectively we felt something was off.

SPIRIT CONTACT

Eventually the intuition you receive and the refined sensitivity to receiving messages, flashes, or subtle energies can lead to spirit contact. You will be able to break down the kind of energy you are feeling into many categories: emotions, psychological states, qualities of relationship, states of health, and knowing when the energy you sense is a spirit or loved one around you. Spirit contact is beyond the scope of this book, but here's a primer in case it is already happening to you.

- ❀ You feel followed or not alone somewhere.

- ❀ You get strong chills in a place where someone has died or when someone speaks of a person who died.

- ❀ You feel protection and love or warmth from a presence.

- ❀ You smell flowers, cigars, or perfume.

- ❀ You hear an inner voice saying your name, or even phrases.

- ❀ You see someone standing in your room at night.

That spirit may be trying to speak to you or through you. It takes a lot more experience and training to navigate this realm. However, if these things are happening and you feel strongly that there is a presence and you feel completely comfortable, you can be pretty sure it is a spirit contact.

❋7❋

PRACTICE EXERCISES AND TRAINING

THERE ARE MANY CREATIVE WAYS WE CAN START to open our intuition. You will need to get a journal and start keeping track of things, and down the road you can go back and read something you sensed and that turned out to have been right.

It's not just about being right, though. We don't open and increase our abilities to have more "I told you so" moments, even though . . . that will happen too. We want to practice and increase our abilities so that we *trust* ourselves in various circumstances. We want to live with a strong sense of self-awareness and trust so things happen more easily in life. We want to know that we can trust ourselves even in the face of adversity.

Here are a few ways to start:

VIBE OF THE DAY

This is a simple but very effective way to start opening and tracking what you sense on any level. As soon as you get up in the morning, before you roll out of bed, ask yourself, "How is my energy today?" Be honest with yourself if you are feeling tired, scared, optimistic, calm, or anxious. Own it.

As soon as you leave your home and hit the route to work, ask yourself, "What is the vibe out here like today?" You can feel it or observe if everyone is rushing, bumping into one another walking, flowing easily, patient, blocked—whatever it is. Now just remember *your* vibe before you entered the outside world.

This helps you start to be conscious of your own energy and to drop into that observer mode of the general energy of that day. If the energies are vastly different, then pay attention to how it affects you and see what insights come. Remember, the more you stay detached and observant, the more you will get intuitions about all kinds of things!

NEW PLACES—NEW FACES EXERCISE

New Places

Every day or two when you can, take your journal with you and go for a short walk or take a detour from your normal habits. Pick one place you haven't been in but feel either drawn to or resistant toward (unless it is for safety reasons).

Before you go inside, ask yourself again, "What is my energy like right now?" Be honest again in as much detail as you can be. It may be something like, "I am in a good mood but feel a headache coming on," or "I have a lot to get done today and my lower back hurts a bit."

Then you go inside this unknown place and just browse or pop in and ask what they do—something quick and easy but enough to feel the vibe of the place. Notice how you feel inside. Notice if your own vibe is getting better or worse.

For example, your headache went away after you walked into a shop. Or your anxiety about getting things done is increasing the longer you stay in a deli. First, notice how the energy is affecting you. Next, you can leave if it's not a comfortable feeling and find somewhere to write everything you sensed about the place. You don't need to tell or show anyone or prove anything to anyone. Just let everything flow out of you. You may be surprised how much detail some environments will bring up.

If it's a local business you visited, you may be able to research the place afterward to see if you picked up on anything accurate. If it was the home of a friend, you may hear something later that confirms what you felt. At this stage, the intuition is just for you—not for sharing with others. It's the observer space, allowing all clair senses to come through with no pressure. It's fun to go on these intuitive adventures. You will get to know your town or city better in the process as well.

New Faces

For this exercise you can keep a small journal on you at all times or record things on your phone as you wish. Whenever you meet someone new—meaning you are introduced or say hello—you take a moment to write down everything you sense about this person. You don't share it; just keep it tucked away for yourself. If you get to know this person over time, you can see if your original intuitions were true. It's not for the purpose of giving anyone a reading, intervening in their lives, or to judge. It's a way to observe how strong your first impressions are, or how much you're able to pick up on without knowing someone. When your intuitions turn out to be accurate, you will learn to trust them. There will always be a certain sensation you feel when you are correct. We have to continually observe and keep track in order to know those subtle signs.

BREAKING NEWS EXERCISE

There's no shortage of breaking news on any given day. If you want to really test yourself and open your clairs, watch the news. When one story or person really grabs you, start recording or writing down everything you sense. Again, this will be just for you, but now you have more chances to research any details you sense.

Years ago a little girl was kidnapped from her home in Toronto. There were no signs of breaking and entering or a struggle. As soon as I saw her, I got a flash of a man standing beside her and felt the conditions of her disappearance. I kept it in mind, and after a year or year and a half the police caught her abductor, and I was right about it. I haven't done enough news cases with research and proof to start calling the police to offer help. This exercise can also be upsetting, so you have to have the chops for it, but it is a great way to practice.

JOIN OR FORM AN INTUITION CIRCLE

When you come together with others who are like-minded, the results are very powerful. The energy of openness and trust in a group helps everyone go deeper and share more than anyone might alone. You can check if there are any groups that meet locally or you can join one online. I host them online and they are very special. Generally it is good to agree on the format and guidelines so everyone shares and is respected during the process. Confidentiality is very important, as is learning how to communicate your intuitive information with sensitivity.

You are welcome to use my guidelines to start your own intuition circle.

I keep groups small—under ten people—so everyone has a chance to share.

We introduce ourselves and take turns speaking. Interruptions are very distracting and not respectful while we share.

I guide people in a short meditation to relax and surround ourselves with light, and I ask Archangel Michael to clean and clear anything in, on, and around us before we begin.

Each person poses a question out loud to the group, and we take a few moments to tune in and receive any intuitions that arise.

We go around one by one and share with that person what we got. The questioner then can give feedback about the information that is correct.

Collectively we *all* tend to have a similar sense. Many times you might agree with what someone else says but don't say so. Your intuition is affirmed when you hear other people saying out loud what you sensed but didn't articulate, and this experience adds texture to the process for everyone.

BODY SAYS YES, BODY SAYS NO

I developed this practice about twenty-five years ago when I was engaged in a lot of inner healing and transformation. There were times I just couldn't arrive at an answer and make a decision and felt I had no one to reach out to who fully understood, so I did this technique that helped immensely. It's great for those times when you feel stuck or can't get out of your thought wheel and into your body.

Lie down on the floor and relax your entire body. It can take just a few minutes or even twenty minutes, depending on the day, to sink into the floor and really know your heart rate is calm and normal.

When you know you are calm, think of the decision that you are torn about. At first, build up the case for yes. If I am not sure if I should move to another city or stay where I am, I first imagine in as much detail as possible that I am going to move to that city. It's a yes. Then I fill in all the things it would take for me to say yes now. You might start to imagine the furniture you would take with you or need once you got there, securing a moving truck, and notifying your landlord or selling your home. Lie still and see how your body feels when you decide yes. If everything in you is seizing up, your heart is racing more, your breathing is shallow, you feel nauseated or have a headache, this is telling you how much anxiety and fear is present with a yes.

Still lying on the floor, come back to center. It may take a few moments. Clear away the yes answer. Feel yourself sinking into the floor until your heart is calm once again. Now we build up the case for a no answer.

If I am not moving to the city, I'm likely staying where I am. I imagine things going on as they have, with no need or pressure to move. Lie still and see how your body feels when you decide no. How do you feel? Does it give you relief, with no outside pressure from anything or anyone, or does it make you feel heavy or tired when you say no?

Your body will tell you how you truly feel on a primal level about your decision. If something makes you spaced out, scared, achy, and anxious in a bad way—your body is saying no. If something gives anxiety or raises your heart rate but also gives you excitement or optimism or a sense of adventure—your body is saying yes, but maybe you have fears about how it will go.

If you feel uplifted, calmed, relieved, or grounded, and solid when you imagine an answer, these are signs of more presence and safety and that is your body saying yes. It's clairsentience on the self in a way, and a very deep meditation. You are also more likely to trust the answer you get because it took you out of your spinning mind and into your visceral senses.

EXERCISES TO DEEPEN

Once you see more and more examples of your intuition being right, and you know how to relax and open and trust it, you will come up to a new layer of experience.

How can you deepen your intuition? You will come up against a new paradigm of life as you live it in action, and this comes with all kinds of heightened experiences, synchronicities, and connections. It also comes with many new challenges. So before you decide you want to go deeper, you may want to consider if you feel ready to really shift the way you live.

Are you ready to pursue your truth and passion even if other people don't understand you anymore? Are you committed to deepening it so you can help others? Are you ready and willing to do the inner work you will need so you can navigate that? I would also say it's best to take this step with support in your life—a group or even one friend who gets you and believes you as your intuition starts to heighten.

What does deepening your intuition look like? It is mainly about the level of sensitivity and awareness you will be operating with. You will see more, feel more, hear more, and just know more about everyone around you.

If it opens quickly, this heightened awareness can be very over-whelming, or it can be a total high. Imagine walking into a bookstore and feeling the energy of all the words and authors on the shelves. Lots of people won't be aware on that level. They will just be shopping for what they want. Now imagine you can feel the energy of each book as you pass by, seeing the author's face on the back and getting a vibe each time as you walk the rows. At the same time, there is a radio playing in the store, people are talking, maybe a baby is crying, and the friend you are with is also talking to you.

Now do you see? Deepening your intuition can feel like this, and you will need to go slowly until you learn a whole new way of navigating life to include and integrate "normal" with the intuitive realm you now experience. This is why many intuitives and empaths don't like crowds or loud noise. We are in tune with our inner selves and want to hear that instead of superficial banter, or a screaming musician.

When you deepen your intuition, it means you will sense more information that is unseen or unsaid. For example, when you see a new couple and your inner voice says, "This is the one for her," leave it at that.

As you deepen your senses, you may find that you see the proposal, envision the wedding, and know the how each person is feeling at each event, and more! Your interaction with the couple will shift because, on some level, they feel your shift and awareness of them. It creates a bond sometimes and other times it creates awkwardness or self-consciousness. The relationship will deepen, or you may see it has limitations. This is true even if you say nothing about your vision to them. And this is a happy vision! Imagine the kind of shift that happens when you see someone's shadow aspect—a pattern they go into when not at their best. You will now interact differently with them—again, even if you say nothing.

Awareness shifts everything!

Before you decide to delve deeper into your clair abilities, ask yourself if you are willing and ready to have your relationships shift, and if you are emotionally ready to receive more information about life that you will carry and be wondering whether to share or not. It is a beautiful path, but it now will take courage and adventure to grow and evolve.

TRACKING YOUR PROGRESS

Keeping a diary, journal, or recordings of your first impressions, flashes of clairvoyance, and messages you hear in meditation or while doing the dishes is an important part of tracking your progress. You will also very likely be clearing a lot of your own emotional issues very deeply as you progress.

This is a new way of life if you are experiencing intuition this strongly, or want to. It's going to mean you are in it for the marathon, not the sprint. Be patient with your process, because it is one of great healing, and your intuition will help you with that healing as well. Spotting patterns, waiting for news stories or people's lives to play out, and seeing if your intuition is accurate, observing what you feel about your own life and are correct about—it all takes time and steady observation.

Tracking your progress and developing a lifestyle in which you are regularly calm and open to listen and heal is the name of the game now. Take some time to decide what kinds of rituals help you in life to stay grounded and open. Buy yourself beautiful journals. Look at what aspects of life are no longer serving your new awakened state, and honor that.

READING PEOPLE WELL

A S SOON AS YOU DETERMINE THAT FEELINGS AND visions you are having of people close to you are correct or give others insight, your life will change. People will look at you differently and they will want more from you. So your first big decision on this path is

Do I tell people what I see?

This ability to "see" has now led you to the first ethical dilemma. Some people feel that if they receive an insight or have a gut feeling that can help someone, they have a duty to say it. They will tell you, "But what if I tell them and this situation can be prevented?"

This is actually a tricky slope: intervention versus allowing things to play out, and who is responsible for the consequences. There is no quick answer. You might hate me for this, but you will have to go with your intuition.

There are certain kinds of things we can tell people that are pretty harmless and either add to someone's life or may bring curiosity, affirmation, or a small warning sometimes. If you had a dream that I was in a beautiful gown at a party and having a great time, please go ahead and share it. It's a hopeful message and may be predictive. Either way, it gives me a lovely vision. If I am going on a first date and show you a photo of the man in question, and you get a funny feeling about him, then yes, say it. Maybe tell me what it is you are sensing about him so I will be aware. My heart won't be broken; it's only the first date. If I tell you I am going for medical tests and you hear, "Second opinion," then by all means share that, because it is always good advice anyway and it may lead to a better diagnosis.

When it comes to more sensitive topics where we are not qualified experts or the information could be very upsetting, we have to use caution and weigh just how important it is. We also have to be fully aware and responsible of the risk in sharing it—either because we could be wrong or because the relationship may not be able to handle this level of truth. I lost many friends in my early years of mediumship, having no clue that others didn't appreciate the truth, even from a caring person. Remember, we are not doctors, psychologists, lawyers, or social workers (even though many people will want us to be when we have a gift!).

I have taken many risks when I felt someone's heart or health was in danger, and I lost some people along the way. Years after the fact, people would sometimes come back and say something—some thanked me or third parties told me I was right. I wanted to protect everyone from everything and have had to learn a lot about this topic.

As a general rule, you have no obligation to tell anyone what your gut feelings or visions are. It's something you received, you can be helpful in many ways that don't involve spitting out predictions. You can act from a compassionate level of awareness based on your intuitive knowing.

If you do decide to share and are coming from a good place—helping someone and being sensitive to their feelings versus your ego wanting to show off or say "I told you so" in some way—then you are safe in sharing it. It will now depend on the how. Many intuitives have put lots of time into understanding healthy communication styles. Doing this can help other people receive your message in the best way possible—if they are able.

AM I RESPONSIBLE FOR WHAT I SEE?

A tricky ethical debate could happen around this question, and I welcome it. If I see that an apple is red, am I responsible for the apple? You are not more responsible for the apple after seeing it than you were previously, but the information has created awareness and that awareness may change you and the apple. You will be altered by what you see, and the apple's vibration will change on some level too, but to me that doesn't imply responsibility.

It may seem silly with an apple, but it makes sense with a person, doesn't it? I see something in you or surrounding you, and now my awareness of you is opened and perhaps changed. I merely see it, but now that I have, am I responsible to help or fix it or warn you of what I see?

It all depends on your values. If I value privacy highly, then I may not say what I sense to someone unless they directly ask me for advice or help. If I value change over other things, I might share it and provoke growth or change. If I feel capable to intervene, then I might share it and stick around to support them, whatever their reaction. If I see life as everyone having their unique lessons that will happen regardless of my sharing my intuition with them, I might keep it to myself. If I feel that a message is meant to be shared, then I will find a way to share it.

When we are truly seen we transform, don't we? If you have a secret and someone sees it, your interactions will be changed. If you are relieved to share it, you may become closer and reveal sides of yourself to them you never shared. If you are defensive about the secret or scared to be caught, now we will see your worst side come out.

This is how the "apple" changes once we see it. When we intuit correctly something in someone or a situation that people are ready to have a dialogue about or bring into the open, we have a window to resolve or heal something. When we intuit correctly something people want to remain hidden or are not able to confront, a lot of covert dynamics appear, and we usually have to make difficult choices on how to act in the situation.

I have met many psychics and intuitives in my life, and we all fall on different points on the spectrum of when it is appropriate to tell people our visions. So the questions I present about suitability are from the vantage point of professionals who have already been there and done that, regarding telling or withholding and the ethical questions involved. Most of us seem to agree that we need your consent before saying what we see. Speaking of consent . . .

9

ETHICAL DILEMMAS AS YOU OPEN UP

WHEN I SEE MEDIUMS ON TELEVISION SHOWS randomly walking up to people and telling them spirits are around them, I shudder. I have been to many public reading circles where we all consent to be there and receive a message if there is one for us, but the ethics of this are questionable to me. We move beyond the debates about whether our intuition is accurate now and into the ethics of sharing it and how it affects others.

BOUNDARIES AND CONSENT

Imagine that you are dealing with a very painful situation in therapy concerning your father, and an intuitive gives you a message in front of others about him and gives advice to you that really triggers you. Even if the information in the message is completely accurate, is it sensitive to present it this way? Is it actually helpful to the recipient? When you first open up and realize your intuition is right, you will feel a high, and you will probably want to share it with everyone because you are feeling your own inner alignment so strongly and clearly, and the messages or visions coming down the vortex are accurate, and for the most part they are well received. Going through this stage is a rite of passage. But in the end, it's not about us. What we share has power, and we are responsible for how we use that power.

Giving random messages in public or group settings is generally not a good idea, because so many people will be triggered emotionally and can feel very embarrassed or unsafe to be that raw in public. When you ask the person's permission first, directly say, "I am feeling something about what you just shared. Can I tell you?" That shows respect for their feelings and establishes their consent and their right to say no.

The way you share an insight with another person can have a huge impact. You are responsible for how you deliver a message to someone. If you are doing it clearly, calmly, sensitively, using nonviolent and nonjudgmental language (an art unto itself), then you are safe to share your insight after receiving their consent. If they are upset after that, the responsibility is also theirs to own, since the feelings are their reaction.

Don't let this scare you away from sharing your gifts with the world! This is part of the mountain to climb, getting the ethics and the wording right, but it's very possible to do, and then you can help people immeasurably! I've been doing it for more than twenty-five years, and it is very rewarding to know I've helped prevent, affirm, and reassure.

CAUSE AND EFFECT

Many people who start having intuitive experiences and seeing events in others' lives accurately begin to shut down. They feel fear and don't want to see anymore if messages they received were sad. They feel responsible. People ask me if they caused what happened because they saw it or because they said it. They shut it all off to avoid the pain and the deeper philosophical or ethical questions.

Let's take an example to explore this. If I get a flash vision of your kitchen as you talk about renovating it, and I see a certain kind of yellow on the walls and you tell me, "Yes! We painted it exactly that kind of corn yellow," did I cause it? If I witness an accident, did I cause it? The answers are clearly no.

If I see that someone is not going to recover after chemotherapy, did I cause the problem? Could I have prevented it by telling them? Again, no. The issue comes up when the things we see, hear, or sense intuitively are about things *we think* could have been prevented. How many life events and choices can be prevented if we are warned? How many life events can manifest if we share our good visions? These are important questions about the nature of reality—and I welcome this kind of discussion, because this seems to be where many fears of trusting and utilizing our gifts come from.

Most of the time you don't cause something by sharing what you see, unless it is unethical to share in the first place. If you encounter an intuitive or a tarot reader telling you when you or others will die or have a tragic accident, get out of there immediately! No one knows the moment someone will be injured or die. These are between your own soul and your creator. So the only time someone can cause something bad to happen when they foresee it is when they share unethical news with a vulnerable person. Always use intuition to gauge what people are able to hear, even with consent.

This is where coaching and counseling skills come in. If you continue to develop your gifts and decide you will share them with others, you will need to learn communication and counseling skills. There are always ways to help someone confront a difficult situation that you have intuitively flashed. You present the information honestly but without alarm. This is one main difference between intuitives and fortune tellers. A fortune teller can be very accurate but usually has no filter, very little awareness of psychology, and is more concerned with telling what they see than with responsible concern for the recipient's reaction and feelings.

Giving false hope is another unethical practice. This could have repercussions in the way someone makes choices and how things then play out. It's normal that people want to hear what you feel or see when they are vulnerable and hoping for a certain outcome, but be honest and don't give false hope. Consider carefully the answer to "How does he feel about me?" when you clearly see it is an abusive relationship, or "I need money. Do you see a job for me in the next month?" If you logically or intuitively feel the answer is no, you can't give false hope or you could be part of creating more vulnerable circumstances for the person. Once again, you will need to be a good coach or counselor.

CONCLUSION

Now What?

Seeing the truth can be a wonderful path, but also a lonely one. Not only do we need our solitude for reflection, rest, self-healing, and processing life, we also spend time alone because we need to be in our truth—and others may not understand our needs or actions. For example, by the time you have learned that many of your visions are not your imagination—they point out something that needs work or repair—you will find it hard to be in the company of people denying and/or not listening to you or their own higher self.

We never want to lose people we care about, so this is the point where many of us start becoming the helpers. We preserve the relationship with someone who we now know we are growing away from (this won't apply to everyone, but you will have some) and rather than set new boundaries, allow the drift, or walk away, we go into help mode. This may take a while, but it usually leads to a very one-sided, service-based relationship because you are not on the same wavelength anymore. Sometimes the other person grows in the same way, too, and over time we restore the equality, but this can be rare because true friendship is also rare.

> **Mysticism is the acceptance that everything cannot be logically explained.**
> —FREDERICK LENZ

As we go within, there seem to be fewer people to share with, but we are a growing community and we no longer have to hide these abilities, so I am more hopeful that the spiritual path won't need to be as solitary as it used to be. Many of us who grew up before the 1990s know that it just wasn't safe to come out with these topics, so to find like-minded people was much more rare then. Still, any mystic will find that they need a lot of alone time and will enjoy their alone time.

What Do I Do with My Gifts?

When I first started this path, most people were in the closet about talking about intuition, visions, spirit contact, and being able to see or predict things. The journey was all about gently helping people overcome feeling crazy and start to share and meet one another. Ten years later, everyone wanted to be trained and develop more. Recently it has all been about "I know I have it. It's happening more and more, but what do I *do* with it? Am I supposed to become a reader? Why am I seeing this at all? What is the path forward?"

There is no one-size-fits-all answer to these questions. If you are someone whose talent is to see, sense, or hear intuitive and correct information, then you are being called in some way to decide if you will answer the call. I didn't go through that decision. I just always felt compelled to share any truth I received in case it helped set anyone free of a fear or limitation. So if you have those skills and are on the fence about the calling, you have some soul-searching to do about whether you feel compelled to use this talent to help others in some way, and how. You also have to soul-search about whether you are well equipped to coach and counsel people directly or if you prefer to bring it into another area of your life. Many businesspeople, artists, musicians, writers, engineers, entrepreneurs, chefs, and others are highly intuitive in their work!

Now What?

I highly recommend developing your intuition for your own life—regardless of whether you ever share it with another soul or not. It is a very high form of self-knowledge and self-trust that will only enhance your life and might possibly save your life one day.

If you decide you want to continue developing your gifts, the next step would be to practice the exercises in this book, meditate, keep a journal, join a circle or form one yourself to meet other like-minded people, and become a calm observer of life.

The more you trust yourself and act on that trust, the more synchronicity, "coincidence," and overall ease and flow you will experience. It will allow you to trust yourself enough to make better decisions for yourself and avoid a lot of pain, conflict, and heartache. It will unlock the mysteries of life. The path of the mystic is there to walk if you choose it.

I hope you choose to experience the magic.

ABOUT THE AUTHOR

Catharine Allan believes that intuition saves lives. The ability to know yourself well enough, calm the mind enough to hear your true inner voice, and discern what to follow is a core strength we can all access. Catharine has been a professional clairvoyant medium and astrology for twenty-five years in Montreal, Canada. She hosts a weekly radio show on www.mixvibezradio.com exploring spiritual/ self-help themes that has 20,000 listeners every week for talk radio along with music. She was a regular feature on JewelRadio 106.7 FM and soon will be on Hits 94.7 FM with her River Rain Energy Report, with weekly tarot and astrology guidance.

Catharine has been teaching intuitive development, meditation, tarot, and astrology for many years with courses she designed, and was asked to teach at McGill University—a win for these subjects, since they were widely banned from universities since the Renaissance. Catharine has been writing a monthly newsletter since 2008 and gives a free weekly Tarot of the Week that is uncannily accurate. She has been interviewed and filmed many times on metaphysical subjects. She also has a YouTube channel with tarot videos for each astrological sign, as well as other subjects.

Catharine practices various healing modalities including Reiki, shamanic Reiki, past-life readings and regressions, space-clearing, medical intuition, and animal communication. She has a background in healing and has independently studied aspects of social work, addiction, mental health issues, and trauma. She gives readings professionally because they can be an important experience and a gateway to other avenues of wellness and healing.

Catharine is also an artist and has worked in professional theater and film as a couturiere and designer of costumes, including Cirque de Soleil. She sang for an Italian wedding orchestra and performs in local charity concerts and cabaret nights.

See an article about *Future Perfect* by Victoria Loustalot at mindbodygreen.org and hear the interview with Jenny McCarthy on Sirius XM. To reach Catharine for a reading or to sign up for her newsletter please visit www.river-rain.com or Clairvoyant Medium Catharine Allan on Facebook.

ACKNOWLEDGMENTS

I would like to thank Victoria Loustalot for her brilliant book *Future Perfect* and the opportunities it has afforded me to have a new platform to talk about spiritual gifts in a real way. I have to thank Kate Zimmermann, my editor, for warmly walking me through the publishing process and for her utmost professionalism. I would also like to thank fellow author Chad Mercree (coauthor with Amy Leigh Mercree of *A Little Bit of Chakras*) for coaching me through the writing process with clarity and wit. Last but not least, I want to thank so many dear friends and clients who have been with me for the twenty-five years I have been giving professional readings and who have supported my unconventional path.

INDEX